The Good Human

9 Radical Practices to Smash Your Ego,
Unleash Your Authentic Self,
and Foster Connection in a Divided World

Dawn K. Hammer

DK Publishing

ISBN: 979-8-9850065-1-3 (pbk)
ISBN: 979-8-9850065-0-6 (ebook)

Cover Design by Cutting Edge Studio
Manufactured in the United States of America

To Padre, for showing me the Path.
To Trinity and Lukas, for teaching me along the way.
And to Jim, for embodying what it means to be a truly Good
Human.

For a deeper dive into the practices contained within
The Good Human, please visit
https://www.subscribepage.com/the-good-human
to download your free action guide and journal.

Contents

Part III: The Arrival

Introduction

What are the traits that make someone *good*? Is anyone ever truly good? Is everyone? And who gets to decide?

I have a definitive list of qualities I believe make someone good: Humility. A willingness to listen before speaking. Genuine desire for peace. A commitment to love for all human beings.

These sound lovely, don't they? Lofty, and worthy of pursuit. But when I reflect on how often I meet the ideals of my self-selected definition of goodness, I must admit with chagrin I fail often. Rather than abiding in humbleness, I'm often full of hubris — especially when it comes to my political and social ideologies. I might appear to be listening to another human, but really, I'm formulating arguments to prove my rightness, then I fan the flames of division rather than graciously bowing toward peace in moments of that self-righteousness. I can't say I'm always committed to loving all human beings, because I have judgments and fears about so many of them that keep me from doing so.

I write this to let you know I'm not a perfect human being. I struggle daily with my ever-shifting ideas about goodness, God, politics, the economy, and my place in the world. I'm not naturally a good and humble human. I must practice, and do real work, to rightfully claim that title.

So must we all.

❁

When I broached the topic of this book to friends and family, the idea was met with resounding encouragement from some ("The world needs this book right now!") and outright skepticism from others ("Isn't the idea of 'goodness' a little subjective?"). My favorite response came from the 9-year-old niece of a friend who, when asked what she thought makes a Good Human, cocked her little head, gazed quizzically at her aunt, and said with a note of impatience, "Why do you even have to ask that?"

We laughed at the utter absurdity of us, as adults, needing a refresher course on how to be a Good Human. But the laughter was quickly followed with a sigh as we each recollected the ugly comments we'd seen written in news stories about brown bodies drowning in rivers as they desperately tried to cross an invisible line into the U.S.; the ferocity with which government leaders were eradicating food and cash assistance from poverty-stricken families; and the racist and bigoted comments unabashedly spewing forth almost daily from some of the most powerful people in the country.

Since November of 2016, when Donald J. Trump was elected President of the United States, I've watched with a growing sense of foreboding as he and his most ardent supporters try to dismantle every foundation we've put in place for a (semi) functioning democratic society. I sit, aghast, as rights and freedoms are systematically stripped from a growing number of brown and Black bodies, women, journalists, scientists, and general citizens. The decorum of respectful debate, and notion that we should challenge ideas rather than attack individuals, seems increasingly impossible no matter which side of the political aisle we sit on. The message I heard first emanating from Trump and his administration and continuing to this day from nearly every facet of society is this: Our humanity is not valued here.

It's that utter disregard for the basic tenets of good humanness I wish to bring back to the forefront of our interactions with one another. We seem to have forgotten, in this age of increasingly bombastic accusations and judgments, how to breathe, give each other the benefit of the doubt, and extend an offer of assistance when a fellow human being is down. My aim with this book is to help us remember those forgotten parts of ourselves. I want us to remember that housed within every human body is an eternal soul just trying to make its way through this crazy thing called life.

❀

I don't profess to be an expert in what makes someone good, nor do I claim to have mastered the art of being good myself. I honestly don't even love the word: There's too much stigma, expectation, judgment, and dogma attached to the idea of *good*. Children are "good" when they behave the way adults want them to. Employees are "good" when they don't demand better treatment. Church members are "good" when they accept without question the ideologies being preached. *Good* tends to elicit ideas of rule-following and approval-seeking, neither of which I personally subscribe to in my quest to become an ever better human.

But *good* seems to encompass the traits everyone unanimously agreed were important for someone to possess to qualify for the title of Good Human: kindness, empathy, honesty, and integrity. No matter their faith, wealth, social status, or economic background, these were the tenets people most often touted as requirements for being considered a Good Human. So here I pause with my own quizzical look: If we're all in agreement on the importance of these traits, *why are we spending so much time spewing hate and fear at one another?*

We humans seem to have lost our way. And I'd like to offer something to help us find the path back.

❦

Before we can take our first step on the path to becoming a Good Human, we need to learn one very basic, very lifesaving tool — breath. This is the foundation, and it's where we'll return, every time, before moving on to the next step: inquiry. We're going to be querying ourselves a LOT in this book. Because despite what we've been told, it's never been about anyone else's opinion or actions; the world emanates outward from that which we first create within ourselves. I'm also going to challenge you to challenge the human beings in your world – gently, and with love – for it's past time we begin brave conversations about difficult things.

This book isn't for those humans unwilling to have their ideas challenged. Nor is it for anyone who insists they have it all figured out. It'll be of no benefit to someone determined to find fault with everyone else while refusing to point that finger back at their own reflection.

By the time you finish this book, I want you to feel *reflective* about your own role in creating the world we inhabit; *challenged* to move through this world differently; *determined* to make changes in your life that will allow you to do so; and *hopeful* that the world both within and outside you can, indeed, be changed. But you won't get there if you don't first make these commitments with me:

iv

Give up, utterly, any attachments you may have to the thoughts, beliefs, and ideological convictions currently propelling you through life.

Listen with genuine curiosity to the needs and experiences of other human beings.

Take ownership over the harms you've perpetrated, knowingly or not.

Elevate the goodness in others and weep alongside them when they struggle.

Recognize and eradicate your racism, biases, and prejudices.

Allow your mind to be changed.

If you're like me — someone who's feeling a little battered and bruised from the fear and hate saturating our social landscapes; are willing to admit you might not have all the answers and some of the answers you thought you did have could be wrong; and are brave enough to dive deeply into some uncomfortable inner spaces — welcome. I look forward to us becoming the very best Good Humans we can be.

May the world be a kinder and more empathetic place because of us.

~Dawn
2021

Part I: The Foundations

1
Get to Know Your Ego

That Voice in Your Head Is Not Your Best
Friend

At the age of 16, you never could have convinced me my thoughts were anything but perfectly correct. I knew in my bones everyone viewed me as a loser. I knew they didn't want me in their world. I knew I shouldn't exist.

At the age of 25, I was beginning to understand my thoughts weren't healthy, but I still believed they were real. I knew they were right. And they told me that an abundant, fulfilled life was unattainable because I simply wasn't good enough for it. I needed to settle for what I had. Anything else was overreach.

Now, at the age of 43, I know the only thing I can know for certain is that I'm not my thoughts, and my thoughts aren't me. I know every moment is a choice between remaining mired in the muck of my thoughts or moving forward down the path of enlightenment. I know the real, Authentic Me is vaster than any of my thoughts could ever allow.

What if, just maybe, this is true for you, too? What if you've been living under a spell, and the time to dispel it is now?

What Is Ego?

Psychoanalyst Sigmund Freud coined the term "Ego" when he established his theory of personalities: Each human being consists of three separate, yet interdependent, identities — the id, superego, and Ego.

In Freudian thought, the id is primitive, unable to distinguish between base desire and appropriate action. The superego gives us our highest sense of morality; it tells us whether what we want is right or wrong. And the Ego acts as a mediator between the two, allowing us some indulgences, yet ensuring they remain within the accepted norms of our particular society.

However, Ego (as I've come to understand and experience it in my own life) appears not so much as the mediator Freud designated, but rather as an imposter: Ego poses as our own voice, has us convinced of its intelligent intuition, and persuades us it's always looking out for our best interests. You know that voice, right? You recognize the timbre and cadence of it. It's been with you since childhood. You think it's your best friend. But what if it's not? What if, instead, it's really your greatest enemy?

The problem here lies with what is genuinely in our best interests. Ego's definition of what constitutes our "best interests" might not actually be in our best interest at all, because Ego's role is to protect us from all it thinks will harm us. But what it believes will harm us is inevitably created by us in the first place, based on traumas experienced in childhood or young adulthood, self-created false belief systems, and superimposed societal and cultural expectations.

Let's say you feel a deep longing to quit your 9-to-5 job and become your own boss. That voice you know so well immediately starts dictating all the reasons you shouldn't: You need health benefits and a steady paycheck. You're not intelligent enough, competitive enough, or creative enough to start your own company. Your thoughts then drift to your past, seeking reinforcement for these warnings: Perhaps you started a blog one time and it failed, or maybe a boss or parent once told you that you weren't leadership material. In the span of just a few moments, that voice you think is your best friend has managed to squash your dream, and you're left thinking the only logical thing to do is continue working a job that sucks the life-force out of you.

Do you see the conundrum? We've made up a set of rules for ourselves based entirely on past experiences that made us feel shame, hurt, anxiety, or fear, and then we've built up a network of what we consider safeguards to keep us (we think) from ever having to feel those ugly things again.

This is what Ego is "protecting." Not us as our Authentic Selves, but rather us as our self-constructed self-images. And those self-images are often not actually serving us, let alone serving the whole of existence, in any sort of beneficial way that inspires growth, change, and healing.

The Two Yous

There are two yous: The one you think you know (Ego), and the real you who exists underneath all the accumulated layers of judgments, projections, defenses, and strategy ploys that Ego has devised for your existence over the years.

The real you is empathic, kind, understanding, and knowing. This real you understands and knows more than that other you, the smaller you, thinks.

That smaller you keeps you contained, riled, and afraid. That you will convince you that others want to take it all from you, everything you've worked for and haven't had a chance yet to earn. This little you is just that: tiny and insignificant and knowing it, so it must scream at the top of its lungs 24 hours a day to be heard amid the clamor of your life.

You pay more attention to this little you because it's the louder, more recognizable voice. In the meantime, real, Authentic You is patiently waiting in the corner for you to remember yourself and return.

Automatic Pilot

Most of us don't realize we have these two different beings inside us. We go blithely through life believing the decisions we make are conscious, that things are being done *to* us instead of *by* us, and external forces are fully responsible for our current level of happiness and equanimity.

We also believe, fervently, that because happiness and equanimity lie outside us, they can be taken away.

It's like hitting cruise control on your car: You're able to relax a little because the vehicle will just keep cruising along at the same speed without you having to exert any effort to keep it there. Maybe you check the side mirrors every so often to see what dangers might be approaching, and yeah, you still need to keep those hands on the steering wheel in order not to drift into someone else's lane, but for the most part, conscious decision making has left the job description.

This is what Ego does. It lets you think you have command over your life, that the most effort it should take to drive through that life is minimal and the reason you have it all under control is because you're letting Ego be in charge. (Actually, Ego's convincing you that you're *supposed* to have everything under control in the first place.)

Ego barks orders — No! Don't listen to him! Or Yes! She's safe! — and we capitulate without thinking because that's what Ego tells us is best for us. Like the Wizard in Oz, Ego doesn't want you to pull back the curtain to see what's behind it. Moreover, Ego doesn't want you to learn there *is* a curtain, let alone question what might be holding it up! This is the only way Ego can keep little you in the world it helped you build.

Here's the thing. At some point, the traffic around you is going to slow down or speed up, a semi-truck will come along and nudge you off the road, or a deer will bound into the highway and force you to swerve. Ego might have you hit the deer at your comfortable steady pace, fly into a rage at the audacity of stupid animals daring to impose themselves on a human landscape, and then sue the Department of Transportation for not creating some sort of barrier to keep the damn vermin out of the road.

Authentic You, however, will notice the "Caution: Deer Crossing" sign on the side of the road, automatically slow your speed, and check the mirrors for surrounding traffic so you'll be better prepared to slam on the brakes when that innocent deer darts into the road in front of you, avoiding hitting it altogether.

Give bigger, more Authentic You the chance to recognize when new situations and ideas arise. Allow yourself to rise alongside to meet them with grace, curiosity, and a willingness to change course.

Fear Monsters

There's no way around it: Ego is a fear monster. It feasts on fear, chews it up into little pieces, and spits them out into your mind for you to nibble on in every waking moment. More than anything, Ego fears its own loss of power should you become brave enough to silence its voice, so it works overtime to ensure you remain too afraid to try. Why is Ego so diabolical?

It isn't. Not really. Ego isn't evil. It's more like an employee behaving badly when they realize they're about to be fired: Ego can feel its time is up, so it throws a temper tantrum to try to keep you engaged long enough to listen. After all, once that Ego employee is fired, what's it supposed to do? Where will it work? How will it spend its time?

The fears our Egos feed us manifest in myriad sneaky ways. Remember how quickly your dream of quitting your job and starting your own company was squashed? Ego convinced you, with remarkable speed and accuracy, that the calling of your soul was ridiculous and unattainable and gave you all sorts of logical reasons to believe in the truth of that presumption. It did so without waiting for you to pause to ask, *Wait. What am I afraid of?* because it knows once you go down that rabbit hole, you'll inevitably discover there's nothing to fear…except that which Ego has invented for you in the first place!

A Shift in Perspective

Let's try an experiment.

Raise your hand in front of your face, palm facing you, fingers spread out wide. Put it right there in front of your nose so that the two touch. Focus solely on the palm of your hand.

What do you see? Say everything out loud. "I see the blurred edges of what I believe to be my fingers and thumb, but I can't really tell what anything is. I can't see what else might be on the other side of my hand."

Move your hand back by six inches but keep your focus on your palm. What can you see now? Say it out loud. "I see my hand in its entirety and can make out the outline of my palm, my four fingers, and my thumb. I see three horizontal creases arcing across my palm and the swirls of my individual prints on the tips of each of my fingers and thumb."

Now shift your focus yet again, this time out beyond your hand altogether. Describe what you see, with as much detail as you can. "I see light dancing across the grass green walls of my office. I see the colorfully painted statue of Buddha that I picked up in Bali all those years ago, perched happily upon the stack of creative writing books that adorn the top shelf of my melon-colored antique secretary desk."

All that happened with our little experiment was a shift in perspective.

When your hand was right in front of your face, pressed against your nose, it's all you could focus on. Your gaze couldn't shift; there was nothing to shift to. It isn't as if there was nothing else to see, but your hand was the only thing you were allowing yourself to see. Your vision was blocked. And it was your own hand doing the blocking.

When you moved your hand back, your worldview opened. You were able to see the hand — your hand — that was previously blocking your view. The impediment was removed, and you were able to now study the impediment itself: You could name it (my hand), you could describe it (four fingers and a thumb), and you could see beyond it (the room in which I sit).

That's all Ego recognition is. You move the hand back, bit by bit, to get a fuller picture. Once you do this, you can see the blockage. Once you see the blockage, you can identify it as, well, an *it*, a thing. And if you can identify it as a thing, that must mean *you are not it*. The "I" you thought you were becomes an observable thing, and you begin to recognize the ways in which it's blocked your field of vision.

What did I just reveal?

You are not your thoughts. Your thoughts are not you. What if this simple-yet-profound wisdom is the get-out-of-purgatory card every saint, mystic, thought leader, and genuinely fulfilled person on the planet lives and breathes?

What if, by embracing this revelation as a law of sorts for how the universe works, we too can become truly free of our fears?

It's only when we arrive at and accept this fundamental truth — I am not my thoughts, and my thoughts are not me — that the real work of separating from Ego can begin. And we must separate from Ego if we have any hope of ever becoming a truly Good Human.

Practice Where You Are, When You Are

Most of us will probably not have the opportunity to live peacefully in the high reaches of the Himalayas in a temple surrounded by nothing but clean fresh air, chanting monks, and never-ending calmness. The real life of most human adults requires navigating a constantly changing stream of demands on our time and attention: kids, friends, parents, siblings, pandemics, politics, finances, church, school, work...

And that's okay. The reality of a busy, stressful life is the perfect environment in which to check our Egos, because in those frustrating, ceaseless moments of rushing from one event to another, or in the monotonous replays of our daily existence, we find Ego most ruthlessly squashing our Authentic Selves. Mindlessness is the Ego's favorite playground. It uses such moments to prove to you the conclusions it wants you to reach: You're unhappy because of someone else's actions. Your world can never be improved. You can't change jobs/leave your spouse/move to another city because you need the money/don't want to hurt someone else/are too shy.

Checking your Ego also doesn't have to involve anyone else. It doesn't require a quiet, zenned-out space. You don't need mounds of air-filtering plants, or floor-to-ceiling windows that let in views of nothing but greenery and open space. No yoga mats, noise-cancelling machines, lotus positions, or perfectly clear minds.

We just need ourselves. Our breath, bodies, and willingness to be better human beings in the spaces in which we already move, the times and places we find ourselves, willingly or unwillingly, currently inhabiting.

Real life is the place where we practice separating our Authentic Selves from Ego. We do this because we're committed to walking the path of becoming a Better Human.

Practice where you are. Begin right now.

❀

You know now that there are two yous: big, Authentic You, and little, egoic you. You understand the voice you've been listening to all your life is not, in fact, your best friend. You've practiced shifting your perspective and accepted why it's so important to be willing to do so: Namely, to eradicate your fear monsters and truly begin living your big, Authentic life.

In the next chapter, we'll dive more deeply into what that looks and feels like. You'll begin to understand the difference in how your body feels when you're operating from Ego and from Authenticity. And you'll learn the single most powerful tool you can reach for, time and again, when Ego rears its ugly head: Breath.

2
Recognize When Ego Is in Charge

Return to Your Authentic Self

In the previous chapter, we learned what Ego is, and what it isn't: It's not, as we've believed for so long, our best friend. Now we're going to learn how to recognize when it, rather than our Authentic Self, is in charge. This recognition won't happen overnight. Just like every other endeavor in life, we must practice new things before we become expert at them. In fact, Ego detection is going to be a lifelong endeavor.

But here's the good news: There's no confession or self-flagellation required when it comes to separating from Ego. It *does,* however, require commitment, a willingness to entertain new ideas and let go of old ones, and genuine desire for change.

After a lifetime of believing our thoughts to be us, it can feel disorienting (and a little overwhelming) to consider questioning every single thought that enters our minds. But for a little while, that's exactly what I'm asking you to do. Because how else will you be able to tell when your Ego is running the show?

There's no magic to this process. It's not a secret recipe that can't leave the family. Thankfully, your body knows all it needs to know to help you uncover the Authentic Self that has remained stifled by Ego. Your job is to simply start paying attention.

Rigid Mind, Rigid Body

A good sign Ego is running the show lies in our rigidity (and I don't just mean our posture, although that can definitely be an indication we're defending against something). Rigidity shows up not just in our spine or the set of our shoulders, but also in our ideas, assumptions, ideologies, and self-imposed rules.

Ready for another experiment? Here's your first self-inquiry exam. Lucky for you, there are no wrong answers:

How are you sitting or standing right now? Are you relaxed, or do you feel tense? *Where* are you relaxed? W*here* are you tense?

For me, rigidity often manifests itself as tension in my jaw and neck. I might realize my teeth are clenched tightly together, or my shoulders are creeping closer to my ears. When I become aware of these sensations, instead of ignoring them, I try to pause and reflect on where my thoughts just were, so that I can figure out what I'm getting so tense about.

It becomes a game of hide-and-seek. Your Ego wants to hide from you every opportunity you might find to see it, drag it into the light, and banish it, so it will cower in ways that seem perfectly normal to us (like recurring back, jaw, or neck pain).

How does tension present itself in your body?

This is a simple question to ask yourself in any moment, in *any* situation, both the ones where you feel perfectly comfortable, and certainly ones where you find yourself feeling overwhelmed, angry, or anxious. No one else needs to be aware you're performing an exercise of self-inquiry: You're simply asking yourself an internal question and noting the response.

If you find yourself thinking, *NO, IMPOSSIBLE, THEY'RE WRONG,* to anything another human being is saying, it's a perfect moment to check that Ego. Ask yourself: *Am I being rigid? Do I **feel** rigid?*

Let's be clear: You never have to agree with what someone is saying or doing. All we're hoping to do here is interrupt the cycle of self-righteousness (Ego!) that has us convinced we already know all there is to know on a topic, that we'll never change our minds (because we don't have to! We're right!), or that the person speaking to us is a complete moron.

Immediately attacking a person (or an idea) by calling them a name or assigning negative characteristics is nothing more than snap judgment, minus wisdom, and discernment. That judgment walks hand in hand with projection, a sneaky psychological defense mechanism we're all guilty of deploying.

Together, they're two very clear signals that we're allowing Ego to automatically pilot our vehicles.

Judge Not

We're all judges. And, too often, we act as juries, bailiffs, and prosecutors, as well.

We judge people before we ever speak to them, based on how they're dressed, the color of their skin, the way they speak or don't speak, the style of their hair, their political and religious affiliations, how they behave in public, how they choose to spend their money, whether they earn any money... The list is never ending.

Every human being is programmed to do this: We see it on TV, hear it on the radio, and read about it in books and on social media. "It" is the social conditioning we've all been subjected to since the moment we were born. "It" is the societal messaging that tells us what's normal and accepted, and what should be rejected.

Here's a question to ponder: Who and what do you tend to judge the most?

For me, it's rigidly strict religious conservatives, no matter the religion. Just writing those words made me grind my teeth. So, you know what I do? I open my mouth wide and let out a good, deep breath. I remind myself that most religious conservatives are simply trying to stand up for ideas they hold dear, that everyone is entitled to their beliefs (and are even entitled to rigidly cling to them, if they want to), and that just because *I* happen to not believe in an idea doesn't necessarily mean it's incorrect.

These aren't easy things for me to do. When I'm confronted with what I consider to be straight-up, good old-fashioned stubbornness or ignorance, my tendency is to want to scream, "We have the Internet, people! There are no more excuses for you not understanding this!" But that's me, judging another person's journey by where I am on my own journey, and projecting away from myself any inquiry that might make me confront my own less-than-ideal tendencies.

I want to make clear here that there is a subtle yet profound difference between judgment and discernment. Judgments are made in ignorance at the behest of Ego: They provide justification for what we want to believe is true of the world. Discernment, however, comes from a place of authenticity, wisdom, and equanimity. We'll talk more about the crucial difference between judgment and discernment in a later chapter. For now, it's important to recognize that judgment feels one way in the body (heavy; smug) while discernment feels completely different (light; curious).

Projection

Sitting on the opposite side of the same coin as judgment is its sneaky stepsister, projection. Projection is the psychological device that allows us to accuse other human beings of being immoral, irresponsible, illegitimate, or any number of other things while denying those very traits are present within us.

How do we know if we're projecting? We're starting our sentence with "you," as in, "You think you're so much better than everybody else." No, friend, *we* think we're so much better than everybody else. Or maybe it's that we really don't feel we're better than anyone else, but we really, really *want* to be. Or perhaps it's just that we wish others viewed us as better than we think we are.

Whenever we accuse someone of something, it's a sure sign that we ourselves are the culprits of that very behavior.

The next time you find yourself in a state of projection or judgment, ask yourself: *When did I last do or say that very thing? When have I wished I* **could** *do or say that very thing?*

Never, Always

"You never listen to me." "They always do this." "He's never going to change." "I'll never be successful." Do any of these sound familiar?

We slip easily into this form of projection, more often than we might want to admit. We *never* and *always* ourselves (and others) to death. If you catch yourself interjecting *always* or *never* into your thoughts or words, it's a sure sign Ego is in control. After all, no one on this planet *always* does/says/thinks anything; no one *never* takes a certain action or feels a certain way.

We're, all of us, ever-changing beings. From one moment to the next, we have the capacity to become brand new: Our cells are perpetually renewing and regenerating themselves. In fact, the person I was when I began typing this sentence is not the exact same being I'll be when I finish it. How cool is that?

A great way to get out of projection and back into authenticity is to flip the script: "*I* rarely listen." "*I* often do this." "*I'm* afraid of change." "I *have* been successful, and I can be so again." This is a powerful trick that can immediately remind Ego who's in charge: my Authentic Me, your Authentic You.

Pay Attention to Your Body

Your body is your best friend, truly. It tells you when you're behaving like a schmuck, and when you're nailing life. Every ache and pain, shortness of breath, spasm, contraction, cramp, cough, or fluttery feeling in your stomach is a hint letting you know something isn't right. You get to turn on your inner sleuth and discover what it might be.

There isn't a right-or-wrong answer to this type of inquiry, but just pausing to reflect when something makes itself known in your body is your best first step to uncovering what Ego pattern might be at play.

Also pay attention to feeling states. Emotions are nothing more than a state of temporary energy. That's it. What happens, though, is that we attach a label to these energy states and then, depending on our relationship to that label, assign a value to it: negative (Scary! Run!) or positive (Safe. Stay). But what would happen if we could simply let ourselves experience the energy state without getting attached to it?

Anger is a huge energy state for me. It's my default when I witness or experience something that feels unjust or unfair. My face flushes, my heart rate spikes, my jaw tightens, and I feel an urge to lash out at something (or someone) physically and verbally. I used to get mired in my anger, staying there for days, rehashing every word spoken and recounting the event to anyone who would listen. Now, I can recognize my anger for what it is: a signal that something feels wrong and needs to change. Then, I can take action to make that change possible.

Sometimes, there's nothing to change, except our attachment to a particular outcome.

I know: Life isn't that linear. And when someone is screaming obscenities at you, outright lying to your face, or you're witnessing or experiencing some sort of abuse or oppression, it becomes a whole lot harder to remember to practice detachment. But this technique is invaluable because it's quick and requires no one else's permission or participation.

You get to return to big, Authentic You, instead of remaining attached to little, egoic you. And that's always the goal on the path to becoming a Good Human.

Hearing Your Authentic Voice With Breath

We understand now what Ego sounds and feels like. We've learned some tools for identifying and differentiating between Ego and Authentic You. But how can you tell when you're moving, speaking, and acting from that Authentic place?

Your first move: Observe the breath.

In my previous life as a massage therapist, I often helped clients settle into our time together by taking three good, deep breaths, consisting of a full inhale to the count of three, followed by a full exhale of the same duration. It was astonishing how many people couldn't take such a slow, deliberate breath. Anxiety would kick in and their breathing would speed up; it remained shallow, stuck in their chest.

One client said to me disparagingly, "I don't need to be taught how to breathe. I've been doing it just fine my whole life." Fair point. But the thing is, she *hadn't* been doing it "just fine" her whole life. What she was doing wasn't true breath because it never moved beyond her chest. That's how dying animals breathe: Shallowly. Quickly. In fear.

Where do you feel your breath? Pause for a moment and take a deep breath. As you let it out, try to picture where that breath started. Not sure? Do it again, but this time, pay attention.

Could you feel it? If not, try this:

Place the palm of one hand on your belly. Place the palm of your other hand on your chest. With your next inhale, imagine pushing the hand on your belly away from your body. Really feel that movement. As the inhale deepens, feel the breath move upward toward your chest and lungs. Feel your chest rise and push against the hand being held there. Pause.

Now reverse it. As you exhale, feel your chest collapse a bit as the breath moves downward. As the breath descends into your belly, suck the tummy in a little bit to really ensure you've pushed all that air out. You can even over exaggerate the movements for a few breath cycles to really get in sync with how this should feel.

When you're first learning to get in touch with your breath (which is really the foremost touchstone to return to whenever you recognize that Ego might be taking over the driver's wheel), this is a wonderful practice to engage with. If you're thinking, *Um, yeah, I'm not doing this in public*, I get it. Practice this at home, behind the locked door of your bathroom if needed to ensure no one else sees you, and get used to how a real, deep breath feels. Then, when you're out and about, running headlong into other people's Egos and responding to your own, you can engage in deep breathing without anyone being the wiser.

Movement Within

Once that breath is moving the way it should, you're perfectly primed for what comes next: Movement. I don't mean, break-into-a-dance-in-the-middle-of-Main Street kind of movement (although, if that's your jam, I'm certainly not going to stop you!). I mean more of an internal movement.

Remember, Ego is rigid. Authenticity, however, is fluid. And that fluidity is something you'll be able to feel as, with your breath, the body relaxes: the jaw loosens, the shoulders come down, the eyes don't feel so tight, the headache goes away. These internal letting-go movements might be massive and alarming — suddenly, you're a big bowl of wobbly Jell-O — or they might feel more subtle, like a sensation of suddenly having more space around and within you. But you'll know when you've hit that perfect moment of surrender because you'll want to say, "Aaaahhhhhhh."

Your body will unwittingly release a sigh as it's allowed to let go. And then...expansiveness, lightness, connection, all the things that were unavailable when you were in Ego will emerge because rigidity, judgments, and projections will fall away. And what you'll be left with is this incredibly calm and peaceful energy state.

You'll be left with Authentic You. It really is like a kind of magic.

We've committed to recognizing when Ego is in the driver's seat by remaining conscious of our rigidity, judgments, projections, and mind and body feeling states.

We know how to breathe deeply. We understand what it feels like to move and speak from a place of Authenticity. We even know how relatively easy it is to get there:

- Breath first, always
- Then, self-inquiry and reflection
- And finally, allowing movement to return

The First Practice: Release Judgments

As you start down the path to becoming a Good Human, you might be shocked to discover how often your thoughts veer toward judgment. If you're a religious person, or consider yourself already enlightened, this might be uncomfortable to come to terms with. And if you're sitting there smugly saying to yourself, "*I* don't judge," then I challenge you with the following:

Pack up a journal and writing utensil. Pick a public spot where there's lots of people coming and going. Sit back and just watch everyone for a few minutes. Then write down answers to the following questions:

Who are you noticing? What are you noticing about them? What thoughts are going through your mind as you observe them? What stories are you making up and attaching to them?

Read what you wrote. What patterns emerge? Did you tend to notice attractive people or the color of people's skin? What stuck out about them? The clothes they were wearing? The conversations they were having (or not having)? What values did you assign to them? Were the attractive people automatically interesting, the people of color automatically threatening, or the White people automatically racist?

There's always something new to discover about ourselves. Paying attention to whom and what we judge and the values we assign to those judgments is a beautiful place to start on our journey to becoming a Good Human.

In the next chapter, we'll explore the importance of asking questions, not only of ourselves, but of others as well. Because we can't be a truly Good Human if we don't engage with the human beings around us, and the most Authentic way to do so is from a place of genuine curiosity. What's genuine curiosity? It's the humble request to be let in through the door of someone else's inner house. After all, isn't one of humankind's greatest needs to be heard, seen, and valued without fear of judgment, reprisal, or attack?

3

The Art of Genuine Curiosity

Asking the Right Questions

By now, you've come to realize that Ego-checking self-inquiry requires, well, an inquiring mindset. In this lifelong work, you'll constantly ask yourself questions to differentiate between your chattering Ego-mind and Authentic voice. As you become more fluent in the language of genuine curiosity, you'll begin asking these questions of the human beings surrounding you, too.

I've only recently discovered the confidence to bravely ask someone why they think their thoughts, believe their beliefs, or idolize their ideologies. For a long time, I was too afraid of confrontation; perhaps I believed any sort of differing opinion had to result in confrontation.

In today's polarized political and social landscape, that's not an unreasonable conclusion. But if we remain too scared to simply ask someone to dive deep alongside us, we're shortchanging both ourselves and them: We're depriving ourselves of opportunities to stretch our thinking and belief systems, and we're simultaneously deciding for another human being that they're too far gone to stretch their own.

Asking genuinely curious questions of ourselves and others is a gift to humanity. Questions allow us to uncover our Authentic Selves, and to authentically connect with our fellow humans. They give us space and time to breathe and reflect.

Genuinely curious questions just might save us all.

The Gift of Time

In moments of unconscious Ego response patterns such as rigidity, judgments, and projections, reminding ourselves to stop, take a breath, and ask a genuinely curious question allows us a moment's respite from the ceaseless prattle of our Ego-mind. Remember, Ego does this to keep us distracted from discerning the truth of our experiences. Stopping to ask genuinely curious questions interrupts this process and allows us space in which to pause and reflect before reaching our conclusions.

It works like this: We get triggered by an event or a person. Ego has us trained to respond a certain way — perhaps with disbelief, contempt, or disgust; maybe with anger or annoyance; or by shouting or with withering silence. Perhaps we want to run headlong into the fray, or maybe our inclination is to run away and not face this experience.

Whatever the unconscious pattern is that's now kicking into overdrive, what we do is *stop*. We take our deep belly breath. Probably one or two more. And then we ask ourselves:

What is true for me, *right now*?

At this moment, what am I feeling? Where am I feeling it? When have I felt this way before? How did I react? What happened to me after I reacted that way? Did I feel lighter, more connected, and recharged? Or did I feel heavy, isolated, and depleted?

At a recent author's conference, a woman in my group seemed determined to be disagreeable. It didn't matter what the topic was; she managed to find something negative to say about each. When we were learning about how to build our author brands with social media marketing, she pointed out that spending time on social media is debilitating for her mental health. When someone suggested she hire a virtual assistant to manage social media postings so she didn't have to spend so much time online, she snarkily remarked how nice it must be to have enough money to do so. On and on.

With every iteration of this woman's negativity, I found myself getting increasingly angry and impatient. The thoughts in my head ran the gamut from, *Geeze, lady, why are you even here?* to *FOR THE LOVE, LADY, SHUT UP AND LET THE REST OF US ENJOY THIS PLEASE!* My egoic self was ready to do what it's always done — retreat into a corner of pessimism and hatred for this woman who was daring to make me uncomfortable at a conference I'd been looking forward to for months.

But then I paused. I remembered our words often let out hints of what our inner dialogues are. And I guessed this woman's inner dialogue might be one filled with fear and self-criticism. And I knew, from my own experience, how uncomfortable that space is to inhabit.

So instead of silently loathing her and shooting her dirty looks all afternoon, I introduced myself. I shared with her my enthusiasm for all I'd been learning the past few days. I told her I got the feeling this conference wasn't giving her what she wanted. She agreed. Then I asked a genuinely curious question: "What's missing for you?" It was genuinely curious because I honestly couldn't fathom how anyone could feel like they hadn't been given a golden ticket to supreme author knowledge. But, clearly, that wasn't the experience this woman was having.

She said she wasn't being given what she'd been promised. I asked her what she'd been promised. She couldn't articulate a precise answer, but our conversation developed from there, with me asking genuinely curious questions and her guardedly responding.

Eventually, I discovered a core belief this woman held: She couldn't afford to implement many of the tactics the presenters were advocating, let alone the accelerator program many of us joined at the conference, and that belief made her feel inferior in some way. Her inferiority belief was her trigger. Her withering negativity was her default response mechanism.

Having been someone who once resented those surrounding me who could afford to do things I couldn't do, I found myself empathizing with this woman. And that was a much kinder place to land than the dark smoldering corner of contempt I'd initially retreated to.

By choosing to engage with genuinely curious questions, I allowed myself — and her — the gift of time: Time to breathe, think, connect, and reflect.

Ask the genuinely curious questions. Allow yourself connection with a human being who is suffering. Extend them the grace you so often crave for yourself. Give them, and your Authentic Self, that gift.

Disrupting Patterns and Finding Clarity

We all have our triggers. For some, it's the way their teenager uses a certain tone of voice when responding to them, one that sounds like disrespectful disdain. For others, it's a spouse distractedly murmuring "Mm hmm" while scrolling through social media instead of listening to them speak about their day. Maybe it's religion or authority. For many right now, it's politics.

Let's say you're watching a political story on your favorite mainstream news station. The topic being debated is one that is near and dear to your heart, one that tends to elicit fiery responses on both sides of the aisle: Abortion. Gun control. Mask mandates. Religious freedom... Pick your poison here. All these topics are ones we instinctively tend to form hardline opinions on, the kind that remain unshakeable. They're often ones we don't remember having consciously decided to have an opinion on at all, let alone understand *why* we hold the specific one we do.

So, fiery newscaster is hurling rapid-fire fiery commentary on [insert fiery topic here]. Chances are, you're doing one of two things — nodding along with self-righteous indignation at the idea that anyone could be so idiotic as to disagree with fiery newscaster's proclamations, or yelling obscenities at fiery newscaster that castigate them, their family members, their pets, and the entire good-for-nothing establishment that sits on the opposite side of the aisle from you.

Sound familiar? Yup. Me, too. It's much too easy to fall victim to these types of mindless reactions. We tend to gravitate toward the orators who are speaking our language, and shy away from (or react violently to) those who don't. This is our automatic-pilot programming, and its power is that it appears quite natural: It's *normal* to feel incensed over someone's clearly incorrect opinion, *especially* when it differs from our own highly educated one.

But it isn't normal. At least, it doesn't have to be — and it shouldn't be the end of our self-inquiry road. Because if we stop at nodding along with or yelling back at someone else's statements, we're failing to discover our Authentic voice, and without that, we're nothing more than mindless sheep being led astray by whatever shepherd happens to be tending us at the moment.

Back to fiery newscaster. As you watch them perform, you're presented the perfect opportunity to question your automatic pilot thinking patterns. You get to ask yourself: **Why** *am I reacting this way?* **Why** *am I agreeing with what they're saying?* or **Why** *is this making me so angry? Is there anything they're saying that's challenging my assumptions on [insert fiery topic here]?* **Why do I find that so threatening?**

If you allow these answers in, you may find yourself feeling mighty uncomfortable. Remember how we learned to sort of tune in to our bodies? Well, now's the time to apply that lesson.

Let's say you've just asked yourself *Why do I find this so threatening?* And you notice as you ask the question you're getting a little squirmy: You feel the need to shift your position, or suddenly have an overwhelming desire to throw the remote or turn off the TV. Instead of indulging any or all these desires, pause. Take your belly breath. Do it again. And again, and again as necessary until those desires subside. Then re-ask the question: *Why do I find this so threatening?* And allow whatever lands, to land.

Maybe you have a sudden memory of your father yelling at his own TV when a newscaster was waxing poetic about this very topic. Maybe you recall a sermon your pastor preached in which it was made clear that to *not* think this way was an abomination of your faith. Maybe your entire family has only ever thought this way and the idea that you might question it feels terrifying to even consider. Or maybe the social circles you're in dissuade this type of transgressive questioning of taken-for-granted beliefs.

Whatever it is, just allow it. Recognize it. Name it. Take another breath. You'll know you've hit on truth when your body relaxes, and you have that "Aahhh" moment.

After that moment is when the real work begins. Once you've let yourself relax into your Authentic truth, you have the blessed opportunity to dig deeper, challenge yourself, and remind yourself that you always have the power to choose anew. To *be* new.

This isn't easy to do. If you're willing to even consider taking this step, I give you props. Personally, I love my opinions and feel they've been hard-earned. And, of course, my Ego wants to convince me that mine are the only logical opinions to have.

But that's the trick of Ego. It's one and only job is to keep me within the confines I myself created so many years ago when I thought I needed protection from things outside me that could cause me harm. But can someone's opinion harm me? No!

There are no right or wrong answers when we're performing this type of self-inquiry. All we're doing is starting to disrupt automatic-pilot responses. We're consciously and deliberately choosing anew, moment by moment. And then choosing to do it again, endlessly.

Bestowing the Gift

It isn't enough to be satisfied with questioning our own belief systems, patterns of thinking, and habitual responses. Part of taking action requires us to step outside ourselves and question those around us, too. Otherwise, we're keeping this life-changing gift to ourselves, and that's plain selfish. After all, this isn't just about *us* — we're out to populate the planet with an entire army of Good Humans!

All the tactics we've learned and are committed to practicing are ones we can (and should) teach others, too. You don't have to be a master to teach; you just have to be practicing. That's all life ever is, after all — continual practice with the expectation that we'll never get it perfect. (If we're perfect, it's time to leave the planet 'cause what else is there to learn?)

What are these tactics that we're teaching to others because we're okay with not being perfect masters ourselves? The art of questioning and the science of allowing.

There's a way to do this that comes off as preachy, lecturing, and paternalistic. That's not what we're after here. We're (hopefully) not talking to ourselves that way, so why would we talk to other human beings that way? What we're looking for here is genuine curiosity. That's it. Unadulterated, unfeigned, Authentic inquisitiveness about how and why someone thinks the way they do or believes what they believe.

My counselor father is a pro at this. He created a process of questioning for working with clients that he calls "Radical Inquiry." It works like this:

Me: "Padre! I'm finally writing my book! I'm allowing myself to indulge!"

Him: "Hmmm. That's so interesting. You said, 'I'm allowing myself to *indulge*'...When did you start believing that to follow your Authentic joy and passion was an *indulgence*? Isn't it actually a *necessity*?"

Several moments of silence.

Me: "Great question. I'll get back to you."

My father didn't tell me my thinking was incorrect. He didn't lecture me on how I should know better by now because I've been involved in this self-inquiry process for so long. All he did was ask a genuinely curious question and then allow me time to respond. What a beautiful gift: He offered me a pearl of wisdom and let me decide whether I wanted to wear it.

When we ask genuinely curious questions of others *without an agenda*, we learn more about their Authentic Selves and, in the process, allow them to meet that person, too.

What do I mean about not having an agenda? You're not entering the conversation with the mindset of a lawyer, ready to pick apart anything the person says without understanding why they're saying it, believing you need to convert them to your way of thinking, or deciding their thinking is wrong and it's up to you to save them from themselves.

Maybe we care about this person and have convinced ourselves they're on the "wrong" path. Maybe we just need to be "right." Whatever the reason is doesn't really matter (although investigating yourself to find out why you're manipulating someone is certainly a damn fine use of time and energy). When we enter a conversation with an agenda, we're manipulating the entire relationship to look and feel the way we believe is best...or at least, to manipulate it in a way we believe will make *us* more comfortable.

But when we enter a conversation with genuine curiosity and empathy — meaning, we try to put ourselves in this person's shoes to understand where they're coming from and why — a miraculous thing happens: connection. We connect in myriad ways with every single human being we encounter along our paths — even the ones we thought were enemies, idiots, or too far gone in one political direction or another to ever bother talking to.

There are dozens of questions we can ask in any conversation that might engender real discourse. The trick, of course, is to be mindful of what questions we're asking, and why. Are we interested in developing an Authentic relationship with this other human being, or are we determined to manipulate them into our own way of thinking and behaving? The answer to this will determine the questions you ask your fellow human being.

Follow the flow of genuine curiosity. Let go of any need you think you have for a specific outcome. Allow this human being before you to struggle with their answers. Be willing to struggle alongside them.

We now understand the importance of asking genuinely curious questions of ourselves and others. We've accepted that to be a practicing Good Human, we need to ask these questions without an agenda. We recognize that to question is to connect, and Authentic connection is a vital component missing from our current social landscape. We're committed to:

- Identifying our triggers and reactions
- Asking questions that allow us time to breathe, think, connect, and reflect
- Bravely asking genuinely curious questions of others, *without* an agenda

The Second Practice: Curiously Question

Recall a time you felt triggered by an event or a person. Re-create the scene in your head. Where were you? Who were you with? What occurred or what was said that created an emotional response?

How did you react? Did you engage with the event or person or did you shy away? How did that reaction make you feel? Tune in to your body. What were you feeling and where were you feeling it? What are you feeling right now just remembering it?

Now, pause. Keep the scene in your head while you take several deep belly breaths. Focus on the parts of your body that feel tense and deliberately relax them. In this way, you'll eventually retrain your brain to react to similar situations in a proactive, rather than reactive, way.

Imagine yourself back in that moment, but this time totally centered in your breath and body. Approach the situation with genuine objective curiosity. From this place, ask yourself what you're curious about: Do you want to know why this other person said the things they said or did the things they did? Do you wonder why you felt so angry/confused/indignant/embarrassed?

Just play with this. Don't get caught up in what should or could have been. Just remain curious about the moment. Try to come up with half a dozen questions you could pose to yourself or someone else should you find yourself in that situation again.

❧

In the next chapter, we'll explore the difference between hearing and listening, and the importance of reading-between-the-lines to discern the truth of what someone is saying. Because we're always revealing the truth of ourselves in the words we choose to speak, and that truth can tell us a lot about where someone is on the path to becoming a Good Human.

4
The Art of Discernment
Authentically Listening, and Listening for Authenticity

Everyone talks. Not everyone listens. I argue that none of us (or very few of us, anyway) can honestly say we fully understand *how* to listen. It's like that client of mine who questioned my sanity for trying to teach her how to breathe: "I don't have to practice listening, thanks. My ears kinda do it naturally. What else is there?"

Turns out, quite a lot. As we now know, most of us are running on automatic pilot, not speaking our truths (because we don't yet know what they are) and not bothering to genuinely listen when others might be speaking theirs.

But they're speaking some version of their truth all the time. We're constantly revealing ourselves with the words we choose to speak, how we speak them, and who we speak them to. Within the first few minutes of engaging in conversation with another human being, we've given ourselves away, and so has the person engaged with us.

If we practice active listening, we can learn who the Authentic being is behind the voice that's speaking. This allows us to ask our genuinely curious questions. And that, inevitably, will foster connection, which is one thing all Good Humans need.

Are You Listening or Just Hearing?

After a long and painful separation from my ex-husband, I came out of my cave of shame and depression and asked two of my girlfriends to lunch. We met at a little cafe on the main street of our tiny downtown. I came ready for good conversation. They appeared with laptops in hand, both talking on their cell phones. And that's how the meal proceeded. One friend received calls every five minutes, smiling and muttering "Sorry" before accepting each one. The other spent minutes between bites typing furiously on her computer, pausing every so often to answer a question I'd posed.

They both apologized profusely and repeatedly, for being *so busy*. They were *so happy* to see me, but they couldn't possibly stop working. I understood, right? No? Well, someday, I'd have my own business or a real job and then I'd get it.

What I got was that I was too unimportant to set aside work for, even for 30 minutes. What I got was that my grief and shame were unworthy of their time and attention. What I got was that I wasn't someone worth listening to.

Their mouths said they were sorry. Their actions belied those words. Had they genuinely been sorry for their actions, their actions would have ceased. If they were genuinely happy to see me, they would have acted like it, by listening actively to

36

my words and engaging with them, rather than ignoring them and focusing on something else.

It hurt my pride to have to admit that people I'd considered my friends clearly didn't consider me the same. But it was empowering to acknowledge the truth instead of pretending the ordeal hadn't unfolded the way it had. And I vowed to never sit down to a meal with another human being with a cell phone or laptop in hand, a vow I'm proud to say I've kept to this day.

How do you engage with or dissociate from the people you say you're listening to? Active listening requires eye contact, head nods, no interrupting, and genuinely curious questions that allow the speaker to dive more fully into the depths of their story. It requires an acceptance that this moment isn't about you but about them.

How do you answer genuinely curious questions when they're posed to you? If you're actively listening to what another human being is asking, you can answer succinctly and authentically, without having to deflect, rush through a response, or ask them to repeat themselves. There's no shame in any of these responses – only opportunities for practice. A good place to start is with a deep belly breath; again, this gives you time to allow the question to penetrate and for an Authentic answer to arise.

Once we begin the practice of actively listening, it becomes a whole lot easier to cut through the noise of the world and tune in to what's actually being said.

Discern the Truth

Have you ever come away from meeting or listening to someone feeling like something was...off? Nothing overtly terrible was said: No racist rants, sexist language, or disparagement of something you believe in. They just left a bad flavor, somehow. You can't quite put a finger on it, but something in you is questioning the sincerity of their words.

Everyone else is responding to this person with unguarded enthusiasm. They're responding to something you simply can't hear. You think there must be something wrong with you for thinking differently. I see this happening a lot with politicians, religious figures, and celebrities: People who have power, and a following, are more likely to hold opinions that go unchallenged (especially by their followers).

Perhaps their words are incongruous with past behaviors. Or maybe it's that the words, as innocuous as they seem on the surface, were said with a sneer that implied the opposite of how they sounded. Maybe they're said with soul-crushing contempt or unfettered hatred.

Maybe there's nothing you can specifically point out that explains your feelings. Maybe that means you need to do a little more self-investigating. 'Cause remember — if Ego is at the helm, it's looking for something to "protect" you from. But if Authentic You is steering this ship, then you know you've found something worth your attention.

On a recent Zoom call, a group of fellow authors and I were in conversation about our current projects. One member of our group was particularly dynamic: smiling, ebullient, and punctuating her stories with mystical words and spiritual phrases. I watched the other participants respond with mirth to her quips and puns while I retreated further into myself, wondering why I wasn't enjoying the conversation as much as everyone else seemed to be. She seemed perfectly nice. She spoke a language I understood. Why didn't I feel connected to her?

After listening and breathing for a few minutes, it finally hit me: The woman wasn't actively listening as we each discussed the beauty and frustration of our writing journeys. She spent more time making assumptions about who we were and what we were trying to accomplish than she did asking us genuinely curious questions about our work. Once I named the unsettled feeling I was experiencing, I was able to rejoin the conversations, doing my part to ask genuinely curious questions about her own project while more clearly elucidating my own.

Of course, you must first separate from your own Ego to ensure you're being discerning rather than just judgmental. If I'd stopped at retreating and resentment rather than breathing and inquiring, it would've been easy to judge the woman's interruptions and assumptions as mere rudeness. But because I remained curious about my own journey, I was able to reach a deeper level of understanding and fully engage in the rest of the conversation.

Respond to What's Not Being Said

We reveal ourselves through the words we choose to speak into the world. Your best friend, spouse, lover, child, parents, pastor, and politicians are revealing their egoic or Authentic Selves each time they speak. Authentically listening means paying attention not only to what's being said, but to the words that remain unspoken.

For instance, how often have you said some version of the following? "I'd love to write my novel/break up with my partner/travel to Europe, but I don't have the time/guts/money?" That qualifier "but" is a giant red flag: It immediately negates what came before it. What are these statements revealing?

In a nutshell: Doing the thing you've ostensibly always wanted to do (or know in your bones you *should* do) is simply not important enough for you to act. *Ouch.*

I'm the first to admit that carving out time to write, bravely ending a relationship, and saving significant amounts of money aren't always easily achieved: They each take work, commitment, and (you got it) action to make those dreams a reality.

But that's the crux here. If you want to write a novel, you're going to have to make the time to do so — no one is going to walk up to you with a handful of magic Time Creation that makes your life any less hectic. If you want out of a relationship, there isn't going to be a perfect time to end it, ever, except now. If you want to fly across the world and aren't currently blessed with financial abundance, you're going to have to decide — perhaps for many months — that your twice-daily Starbucks Frappuccino habit is less important than your vacation savings account.

When people tell you they don't have time for or can't afford something, you can challenge them (lovingly, kindly) with a simple question: "What *do* you have time/money for?" This does two things: it reveals you're paying attention to what they're saying (and not saying) and, more importantly, it puts the onus on the speaker to explore their statement more thoroughly. Meaning, whether they like it or not, you're inviting them to really reflect on what they've just said: If they don't have time for things that would bring them joy, what on earth *are* they making time for?

This is a great question to start by asking yourself. Get a little uncomfortable with the answer. We all want something other than what we have. And we're all making excuses as to why we can't have it. What do *you* have time and money for?

Unspoken words show up in all sorts of ways. Think of politicians, religious leaders, lawyers, newscasters, and public relations specialists who make a living carefully selecting words to make us believe in their version of a story. It often isn't what they say that helps solidify our opinion; it's the implications made by what they deliberately leave out. They leave us to fill in the blanks, and those blanks are inevitably filled by what our societal programming tells us should be there.

Think of how politicians make a habit of publicly criticizing how expensive implementation of a new program the *other* party is advocating will be while refusing to transparently state how much money *they're* spending in other areas. By focusing their critiques on the other party, we, in turn, are guided to ignore the potential misdeeds of our own.

This is the moment we pause. We reflect on the words said, the ones tripping us up. We conjure them like a magician pulling a coin from a naive child's ear: We examine the trick and uncover the mechanism they used to produce it. We study the words spoken, consider the ones left unspoken, and genuinely question the meaning behind both.

Sometimes, we must do the hardest thing of all — act on our hunches, which might mean confronting someone who's speaking inauthentically or challenging someone's support of that person. Not every situation requires such a confrontation, of course. But if it does, we must be willing to let someone go — or let their ideas go — once we realize their words are consistently inauthentic. This becomes more difficult with people who hold power over us: It's easier to dismiss a casual acquaintance who hasn't told the truth than it is to question the veracity of our pastor, our parents, or our political party leaders.

Listen carefully for unspoken words. Ask genuinely curious questions to guide them to the surface. There's almost always so much more that needs to be revealed before we can say we've fully arrived at truth.

Cultivate Connection Instead of Fomenting Division

To be a genuinely Good Human — not society's version of a "good" human or your parents' or your kid's, but a good and humble human who adds to the beauty and unity of our global community — means to become a master of the art of discernment.

At times, we need to stand up and speak out. In this time of social turmoil, those instances occur frequently. But at other times, speaking up just isn't going to be fruitful.

Let me be clear: There's *never* a time when speaking your truth, with your Authentic voice, from the space of big You, is remiss. There *is* a time, however, when Authentic You is so far removed from the ears surrounding you that to speak would be to engender more harm than good.

For instance, does it make sense for me, a self-described democratic socialist, to attend a rally for Donald Trump and logically expect to sit down and have a meaningful conversation about my belief for government welfare to shift from corporate entities to human beings, and expect the topic to be rationally engaged with, listened to with empathy, and responded to in kind by the people in attendance? No. That scenario doesn't make sense. All I'd be doing is adding fuel to an already roaring fire. I'd be inciting more division, not cultivating connection. And genuine connection with our fellow human beings should always be at the forefront of our interactions.

However, if I'm chatting with my long-time friend who traditionally votes Republican, and she's arguing that Trump's presidency was "good for the economy," I can kindly-but-firmly disagree, offer my rebuttals in dignity and kindness, and work to create the kind of change I'd like to see in my world by actively engaging her in real dialogue, one where I ask genuinely curious questions and listen actively to her responses.

In fact, if I'm committed to being a Good Human, it's my responsibility to do so — assuming, of course, that I practice what I preach, by breathing, tuning in to my body, squashing my Ego, speaking from a place that's genuinely curious about her beliefs, and embracing a willingness to be separated from my own, should the need present itself.

We never need to agree with someone to hear them. We don't need to change minds and hearts. We just need to show up, listen actively to what our fellow human beings are saying (and not saying), and remain genuinely curious about what they're sharing. That's it.

Isn't this what you want for yourself, after all, to be genuinely heard without fear of judgment or reprisal?

Inquiry in Real Life

Let's return to that conversation with my friend who devotedly votes Republican. When she says to me, "I don't like Donald Trump, but he's a great businessman. He helped turn this economy around," I can take my deep belly breath, then ask her a genuinely curious question: "You say he's a great businessman. Can you tell me what you mean by that?" or "I hear you say he 'turned this economy around.' What does that mean?"

Nothing more. I'm not trying to steer the conversation in a particular way; I don't have any agenda other than to understand what my friend means when she says certain things.

A crucial aspect of this type of inquiry is a willingness to admit when I don't know anything about the topic at hand, such as, in this case, what Donald Trump did or didn't do for the economy. Because my Ego is no longer running my show, I can admit when I need to learn more, rather than just jump headlong into an argument about a topic I don't yet understand.

What I *can* say to my friend, from a place of genuine curiosity, is this: "I notice when you say he's a 'good businessman' that I stopped breathing a little. My jaw is tight and I'm having to consciously work to take a deep breath. I just haven't seen any evidence to support that statement. Honestly, even if it were true, I'm not sure that has anything to do with being a good president."

Who knows how the conversation might develop from here? Perhaps we'll begin debating the role of government or discussing the need for a metric other than jobs reports to measure how our economy is doing. The point is that I'm engaging with her differing opinion in a meaningful way which might just bring the two of us to a place of shared understanding and, therefore, connection rather than division.

We're presented myriad opportunities to stop Ego in its tracks, to choose instead to actively listen, ask genuinely curious questions, and foster connection with our fellow human beings.

Always, we start with breath. Then, we move to self-inquiry:

- What am I feeling? Where am I feeling it?
- When have I felt this before? What similar circumstance have I been in?
- What was the outcome? Is it one that fostered connection, or one that caused division?

- What's a different way of approaching this conversation or situation that I've never tried before?
- What questions can I ask of myself or this person to gain clarity?

Amid debate, attack, or heightened emotions, ask yourself:

- What is this person revealing to me? What can I mirror back to them?
- Do I need to continue the conversation, or should I disengage?

And once the encounter is finished, reflect on the following:

- How am I feeling now? Am I elevated, uplifted, and enlightened? Or am I depressed, dejected, and remorseful?

The Third Practice: Actively Listen

The next time you're engaged in conversation with another human being, practice active listening. It doesn't matter who the person is or what the topic is about. You can practice with your child, your partner, your coworker, or with the person who's bagging your groceries. It can be a two-minute conversation or a deep dive into something more substantial.

Your goal is to stay quiet while they speak. Look them in the eye and don't look away. Don't think about what you want to say when they've finished speaking; don't interject with a story similar to what they're sharing. Just listen.

When they've finished speaking, keep the focus on them by asking one genuinely curious question, one that can't be answered with a simple "yes" or "no."

It can be uncomfortable at first to silence ourselves and let another human being fully engage with their stories. It can feel awkward to pay so much attention to someone else without allowing our gaze to wander. But it's necessary. Active listening short-circuits the faulty wiring of Ego that says no one else in the world is as important as we are. It's one surefire way of building bridges of connection over the chasms that divide us.

※

By really taking the time to reflect on our interactions with others, we can determine who should be allowed to remain in our circles. If someone is constantly leaving us feeling depleted, that person no longer gets access to our heart and mind: They've lost their privilege.

This doesn't mean we only invite into our circles those whose ideas already align perfectly with the worldview we want to desperately cling to. It means we're selective about who we engage with because, while it's admirable to seek out those who challenge our thinking, it's *never* required that we spend time with people who humiliate, demean, dismiss, or in any other way harm our Authentic Selves.

As we'll learn in the next chapter, if we ourselves are the perpetrators of harm based on our own ignorant assumptions, presumptions, judgments, projections, or beliefs, then it's past time to face those ugly facts, take real ownership over the harm we've caused, and do the work to change.

Part II: The Work

5
Don't Apologize. Take Ownership

Walk Your Talk and (Really) Don't Do It Again

We've all screwed up. We'll screw up again. It's inevitable — we're human. What we're trying to embody here is the idea that we can do this *better*. And the first step in the whole messy process of becoming a genuinely Good Human is understanding how to acknowledge harm once we've caused it, and then actually *do* something about it...which is entirely different from issuing a back-handed apology and then running out into the world to quickly repeat the foul.

Acknowledging Harm

My teenage son and I have a sometimes-fractured relationship.

All teenagers rebel. But this one has made it into fine art. He knows just when to push my guilt buttons, when to deploy sneak attacks, and when to retreat into sullen silence. He's my son, after all — the apple doesn't fall far from the proverbial tree.

After a late-night pickup from a friend's house, my son informed me he'd forgotten his backpack at another friend's house, and we'd need to drive there to pick it up. At 11:34 pm. On a work night. I took a deep breath, let him know I was frustrated he'd forgotten the backpack, but acknowledged we all forget things sometimes and agreed to pick it up. Along the way, he deftly maneuvered the conversation to one of his favorite guilt-inducing topics: driver's education (specifically, the fact that he hasn't been allowed to take classes to get his license yet).

I did my best to engage the conversation in a way that honored his feelings (angry with me for enforcing what he thinks are insanely stupid rules) while firmly reiterating why those rules were in place (his willful neglect of All Things School). His voice became louder, my jaw grew tight, and finally, the explosion occurred: I ended the conversation by proclaiming him to be ungrateful and a burden to the people around him.

The silence was immediate. My son's pain was palpable. But I was so wrapped up in enumerating (in my head) all the ways he'd wronged *me* that I couldn't hear or feel it. Because I was so committed to making myself the victim in that exchange with my son — after all, he'd said some incredibly mean and hurtful things — I was able to justify why I'd said what I did. I told myself he deserved it; I told myself it was true. I refused to pay attention to his silence or acknowledge the ache forming in my own throat.

We've talked a bit about how important it is to pay attention to signals our bodies send us. Well, harm caused to others leaves an unmistakable flavor in our mouths and sickness in the pits of our stomachs. You know exactly what I'm talking about: It's the feeling that makes you shift from one foot to the other. It makes you look away from the hurt in someone else's face. It makes you squirm.

And then, if you're like me, maybe you get pissed. After all, who are *they* to make *us* feel guilty? We don't need to feel badly — they *made* us do this! If they hadn't been driving so slowly/staying out past curfew/too lazy to work, we wouldn't have had to lay on our horn/scream unintelligible things/vote to eliminate welfare.

As quickly as that, here we are, right back in the warm, familiar embrace of our Ego. It's always there, waiting for us with open arms, justifying any action taken or words spoken, no matter the level of harm we may cause. Because Ego's job is to protect our little selves that we created in unthinking, unconscious moments — not elevate our big, Authentic Selves to a place of empowerment and unity.

But we know better now: That voice in our head is not our best friend.

Take a Breath and Look Them in the Eyes

Here comes the hard part — confronting the pain we've caused.

This part sucks, royally. I'm never smaller than when I must look someone in the face and acknowledge a hurtful thing

51

I've just said or done (and that's saying something — I'm only 4 feet 11 inches tall).

But here's the wonderful, magical part of sitting in our shame-and-guilt-filled muck (and, if we're properly apologizing, which I'll get to in a minute, we *should* be feeling shame and guilt...albeit only temporarily): Once we take that breath (because it always, always starts with breath), open our mouth, and speak the words, "I know I've caused you harm," then this amazing, momentous thing happens.

We connect. The person across from us gets it, that connection. They understand, intuitively, that we see and hear them as another worthy human soul on this chaotic planet, that their value is inherent in this very simple fact: We value them and our relationship. We'll make the time and create the space to take responsibility for our actions and strive to make amends.

Apologize, And Mean It

You've heard the saying, "Walk your Talk." Well, like most charmingly enduring phrases, this one is worth repeating.

About one week and several strained encounters later, my son and I had the conversation we should have had immediately following my harmful statement. He looked me in the eyes and shared how my words made him feel (unwanted, unloved). I looked him in the eyes, listened without interrupting, acknowledged the hurt he said my words caused, and told him truthfully how sorry I was that I said them, because they weren't true.

I told him those words were reactionary, said out of frustration, exhaustion, and my own hurt. I asked him to please let me know immediately the next time I said something that harmed him in any way so I could address it in the moment. And I told him I would continue to work on my own reactivity so that even difficult conversations wouldn't devolve into accusations or arguments. Then, I asked him to forgive me.

There are apologies, and then there are meaningful and impactful apologies.

The words "I'm sorry" aren't an exoneration. On their own, they do nothing to rectify harm. (As an aside, one word of advice here: Never, ever, under any circumstances whatsoever, add "you" or "but" to an "I'm sorry" statement, as in, "I'm sorry you don't understand my point of view," or "I'm sorry, but you really made me mad." Just — No. Never. Not acceptable. Ever. That, my friend, is totally manufactured bullshit — *not* an apology).

A proper and Authentic apology sounds like this:

"I'm so sorry for [insert action or word here]. I understand this caused you harm. And I take ownership for that. I promise that next time, I will [insert totally opposite action or word here] instead. Please forgive me." We could add an expression of thanks for allowing us the opportunity to apologize. If it's someone we love, this is a perfect time to tell them so.

It's important to ask for forgiveness, because the word "sorry" in our lexicon is so overused it's lost all meaning; on its own, it can feel flippant. However, when paired with the acknowledgement of the specific harm we've caused and a genuine plea for forgiveness, our apology opens the door for wounds to be healed.

It's equally important to remember they don't *have* to forgive us. If we've caused harm, we take responsibility and do something to improve. End of story. If they do forgive us, that's icing on the cake, baby. The real success to celebrate here is us stopping and acknowledging our words or actions that harmed another human being and being genuine in our conviction that we can and *will* do better next time.

Take Ownership

The final step in any Authentic apology is to take ownership. And if you're thinking, *I just did that, didn't I?* the answer is no. You're not done yet.

Taking ownership is taking action. This is perhaps even more difficult than allowing ourselves to wallow in the dirty muckiness of shame and guilt after we've royally screwed up because it's something we'll have to remember soon.

Long after the icky feeling has dissipated, and long after the sort of glowey, sunshiny feeling of having acknowledged the harm we caused has faded, we'll be faced with this very same experience again. This is how life works. We make bold promises to ourselves, God, our kids, and our dogs, and then we go back to being our little egoic selves, responding to things the exact same way we always have, falling back into our created Ego patterns, living a supposedly easier life.

Don't let this happen. When — not if — you find yourself facing the same circumstance, *choose* to react differently.

I know, I know. Easier said than done. But completely doable.

Choose Anew

Life is circular: We find ourselves in a scenario and react to what we think the scenario is telling us; we go about our merry way (or maybe not so merry, as the case may be); then, like clockwork, the same scenario appears before us again.

Here, we have a choice: Do we react the same way with the inevitable same outcome? Do we really want to have *Groundhog's Day* over...and over....and over again? In the film, Bill Murray's character re-lived his own self-created hell endlessly. We don't want that. We want change. We want growth. We want expansion. Well, the only way to expand is to (you guessed it) breathe. Take that deep belly breath you now know how to take. Take another. And then one more. You can do this in the space of a few seconds. You know what those deep belly breaths give you? A severing from your ingrained reactions, and time.

With this gift of time, what are you going to do? Are you going to squander it with what comes "naturally?" That "naturalness" is nothing of the sort, you now know: It's the conditioning along the ostensibly easier path that your Ego wants you to stay on to be (as it will tell you) protected and safe. Ego will tell you to ignore the harm you've caused; it will tell you your guilt is unfounded. It thinks you're better served by avoiding having to feel uncomfortable.

You know now this is false. The breaths you take will give you the time to remember what Authentic You already knows:

only by jumping into the muck are you afforded the opportunity to wash yourself clean.

So, no, you don't squander this opportunity, this gift from the universe that's allowing you another chance to choose again, choose anew, and walk a different talk. You take a deep breath and dive into the uncomfortableness that comes with behaving differently after offering an Authentic apology.

Take a Breath, and Remember Last Time

These precious few moments of breath also give you space for inquiry. Remember, we're always asking ourselves questions, opening to the curiosity of our existences: Why do we think what we think? Why do we do what we do?

In this moment of repeated experience, we get to ask ourselves: What did I do last time that caused harm? How did that harm make someone else feel? How did *I* feel when I had to sit in my muck and acknowledge that shameful harm? Do I *really* want to do that again?

If your answer is, "Screw it. This person is horrible/I'm really pissed off/I couldn't care less about hurting myself or another human being," then okay — have at it, brother. You do what you want; you have the right, of course. I'll be over here refusing to bang my head against the same already-bloodied brick wall, breathing through your pain and frustration, and going along my merry way.

I hope you'll decide to walk alongside me.

Recognize the Trigger

Overwhelming emotions don't just appear out of thin air. We create them, for one thing, when we choose to react to what are otherwise neutral events, and we *allow* them to exist. It stands to reason, then, that we can also disavow them. Here's what I mean by that.

Let's return to the moment when I told my son he was ungrateful and a burden. What precipitated my words? Well, my son yelled something about how I always do this — I refuse to hear him when he speaks, I act like I'm better than him and everyone else, and I enjoy controlling him...just like his dad does.

My choice at that moment: to be angry or not to be angry. My opportunity at that moment: to recognize my trigger.

Was it just that it was 11:34 pm, and I was tired and grouchy? Was it that my son was being disrespectful and unkind? Was it that he was projecting onto me his own sense of self? Maybe it was all those things. But if I'd been brutally honest with myself in that moment, I'd have acknowledged there were two dynamics at play triggering me to respond reactively and unkindly: My son equated me with his father, my ex-husband (whom I consider to be manipulative), and there was truth to his accusations (I *don't* always listen; I *do* sometimes consider myself better than other people; I *do* like to control things).

My Ego didn't like either of those dynamics because they confront the image we've carefully constructed together: That I'm a good woman who's forgiven her ex-husband, always listens actively to people she claims to love, never judges other people, and goes with the flow.

There are always triggers, and they're rarely what we think they are. It takes some investigating to uncover the kernel within the husk.

Take a breath and ask a question. Dig deeper. Respond differently. Try it just once, and you'll feel the difference.

All emotions are a choice. All reactions are a choice. How do you want to exist in the world?

The Fourth Practice: Recognize Triggers

Think back to a time when you reacted negatively to a person or situation. Negativity presents itself in myriad ways: anger, frustration, impatience, withdrawal, silence, yelling, passive aggressiveness, gossip, hostility, name-calling, deflection... All of us have a particular style of defensiveness, just as we all have triggers that make us feel the need to defend ourselves.

Recall that moment of negativity. What was the precipitating event? Were you watching the news? Fighting with your spouse or child? Angry about something your boss said or did? Home in on the specifics: Who said something to you or what did you witness or experience in the moment you lashed out or retreated?

Take time to explore the instant you decided to engage Ego's game of self-defensiveness. Take a breath and create space to discover *why* you decided to do so. What's the payoff you receive for choosing to be angry, withdrawn, sullen, or rude? Do those experiences keep you from having to delve further into Authenticity, where it might feel uncomfortably unknown?

There's always a payoff for choosing to remain stuck in Ego consciousness. What's yours?

❧

We've learned how to breathe. We know the types of questions we can ask ourselves and others to ascertain the proper course of action. We know to look for triggers and understand that our responses are *always* a choice. So now, it's time to walk through the world, not just a little bit differently, but as a completely new being.

We do this by actively living the values we preach, honoring the promises we've made to those we've hurt, and being engaged in the work of self-discovery. We do this by not just speaking words we think others want to hear (which is the purview and perfection of Ego), but by speaking words and taking actions that are in alignment with our Authentic Selves — your bigger You. My bigger Me. Together, we take the world by storm.

Ready to put into practice all we've been learning? The next few chapters dive deeply into some potentially triggering topics — namely, the inherent racism our nation is founded on and the requirement that we drop our devotion to ideologies if we truly want to walk through the world as Good Humans. Get ready to swim.

6

In Order to *Be* Good, We Have to *See* Good

Witness the Beauty and Grace of Other Human Beings

It's easy these days to feel overwhelmed with — and saturated by — the negativity of it all: Divisive politics. Hateful rhetoric. Alarmist news headlines. A dangerously warming planet. Worldwide pandemics.

No wonder we're all overworked, overstressed, and overly tired. I don't know about you, but the more negativity I experience the more apt I am to pay attention to all that's out there. It becomes a self-fulfilling prophecy: The world seems to be filled with nothing but toxicity, so all I see is toxicity. And since toxicity is all I can see, that must mean the world is filled with nothing but it, right?

Wrong. The problem with this type of circular belief system is that it becomes almost impossible to differentiate between the truly terrible things that occur in the world and the stuff that's just everyone else's drama, which we can choose to engage with...or not.

Instead, we can choose to bear witness to all the good in the world. Once we focus on that, something miraculous occurs: We begin to see it every day. And the more we do, the easier it becomes to believe in the goodness inherent in ourselves and other human beings, too.

Everyday Miracles

I got the idea for this chapter on a blisteringly hot day in Washington. Just, God awful. The type of heat that makes asphalt shimmer and humans turn on each other in zombie-apocalypse style about such insignificant things as missing out on the last box of organic strawberries.

After escaping from just such an encounter at my local grocer, I walked outside into the baking heat to discover the car next to me was parked so close I couldn't open my driver's side door without banging it into their passenger side. After serious contemplation about whether I would do so (scratch on my door be damned; they needed to be taught a lesson!), I heaved a sigh, stomped around to the other side of my car, tossed my groceries in the back, and slid my sweaty bum across the sticky black seats, cursing with every holy name I could think of whoever the owner of the car was who had the freakin' audacity to park so unnecessarily close to mine.

As I hefted myself over the console and into the driver's seat, I glanced up to see a beautiful thing. A young woman was half bent over a frail-appearing elder, one hand on the older woman's arm to steady her, an encouraging smile on her face, blonde hair falling in a cascade as she edged downward toward the tiny older woman, who was visibly shaking as she lowered herself into the younger woman's waiting car.

I was instantly struck by the nobility of this gesture: One human being taking the time — however long that time might take — to help another human being with a task they could no longer safely do on their own. I have no idea if the woman was a daughter, granddaughter, or paid caretaker, but the patience and kindness etched on her face was something I couldn't dismiss or look away from.

She wasn't ingratiating. There was no grimace under her smile, no hint of hope that this all move a little faster. She was just there in the moment, for the entirety of the moment, with nowhere else to be but there beside this older woman, offering her assistance in whatever way she could. Suddenly, it didn't matter in the slightest that a few humans had annoyed me. All that mattered was the example of this woman who clearly valued another human being so much that she gave her time, energy, and attention to that one so she would know she was seen and valued.

I walked back into the store to buy a bottle of water and sandwich for the houseless person who always sits on the corner by the entrance of the grocery store. I asked for $20 in change and tucked it in with the napkin. I have no idea what that $20 was used for; I don't think it matters, since I chose to gift the money. I also chose to *see* this person, rather than just looking at them and then quickly away, and offered something admittedly small I could share. I hoped the gesture would lighten this person's load, even if only for the time it took to eat a sandwich and drink some water.

There's more I could've done; there's always more. I could've engaged the person by asking what she needed that might help her get off the streets. I could've listened actively and with genuine curiosity to her story.

By bearing witness to the young woman's kindness, I was inspired to practice some of my own. As I stopped focusing on the other human beings who were being a little thoughtless that day, their power over me ceased to exist.

This, too, is a type of magic. And we can possess it any time we wish. Why ever choose otherwise?

Elevate the Good, Holy, and Beautiful

How do you spend your time when engaging with others? Think of the hours spent on social media. What type of information and conversations are you seeking out and paying attention to?

Now think about in-person gatherings with friends, family, or coworkers. What are the topics of conversations? We spend a lot of mindless time in perpetual negativity: We're denigrating the latest opposing politician's efforts to suppress this or endorse that. We're ruing the latest school shooting, police killing, protest, tax hike, or tax cut. We're gossiping about so-and-so's impending divorce or pregnancy. We're complaining about our kids, spouse, boss, or life.

Sometimes, we want to vent, get it out of our system, get others on our side, or just feel heard and seen. But at what cost? Negativity begets more negativity. Every time.

Now, what if we could reverse that? What if by choosing *not* to engage with the doldrums and drama, instead choosing to elevate the good, holy, and beautiful, we created more of those things for ourselves and the other human beings around us?

I admit some things suck royally. Real pain exists in the world, which needs real saviors to help eradicate it. There's racism, abuse in too many forms to name, exploitation, suppression, oppression, and abandonment. We suffer trauma. It's deep and feels insurmountable. I don't want to ignore or wish away these very real experiences. But we *do* have a choice in what we elevate. We can uplift the good, even amid the negative.

Yes, we need to be in conversation about hard things. We need to create brave spaces where such conversation can take place. But within that space there's no room for gossip or meaningless, mind-and-soul-numbing negative chit chat. What there *is* room for — what is required — is deliberate, conscious, fulfilling dialogue about what might be wrong, so that we can work together to find solutions.

We look for the good. We honor the holy. We uplift the beautiful. We choose this, over and over again, until it becomes our new habit. In turn, we ourselves become these very things, and we sprinkle these new bits of ourselves over the Earth as we walk.

Be Still, and Marvel

It's almost impossible to see good when we're rushing around like crazy chickens with our heads (and hearts) cut off from our bodies, unable to stop and smell the proverbial flowers.

We must get better at practicing stillness. We must learn to be okay with the at-first uncomfortable sensations that arise when we become quiet. Because they *are* uncomfortable in the beginning. Our society doesn't value stillness. It labels such moments as laziness, selfish indulgence, or wasting time.

I refuse these labels. I can't be a Good Human if I don't stop moving long enough to explore what that phrase means, to excavate the places where my goodness has not yet surfaced, and work to bring those bits to light. While a slothful life is indeed something I'd consider wasteful, a life spent cultivating moments of complete stillness in order to breathe, see, hear, reflect, and grow is the exact opposite of wasting time: It's time well spent because it leads us to places we never would've known had we continued rushing through life with no time to experience them.

I lived in Washington state for nearly 30 years before venturing out to explore her wonders. I spent my time housed in a body full of shame, fear, and boredom. I filled hours with alcohol and drugs; then babies; then TV, movies, food, and mass consumerism; then depression and withdrawal. I'd find anything and everything cheap and easy to pass the hours, no matter how monotonous and mundane they made my life.

Once I emerged from my self-created bubble of unhappiness, I discovered the magically healing power of nature. I began hiking, spending time on longer trails, moving higher into the mountains surrounding my home, venturing far from the town I'd known since childhood, learning the importance of shutting off technology and the voice in my head that had *never* been my best friend.

I've found the most peace and contentment in the quietest of moments that come just before sunset and again before sunrise on a mountain peak, where there's nothing available to distract me from myself, and the only sounds are critters scurrying nearby and birds swooping and singing in the clear, crisp air around me. I don't bring headphones. I allow nothing but myself and what nature has to offer.

In those moments, I'm closest to Authentic Me. Also, in those moments, I'm furthest from the madness of the world you and I cocreated, the one that wants us to remain divided, afraid, and unhappy. That's no coincidence.

You don't have to struggle up a hillside to find this stillness. You don't even have to go outside (although if you're fortunate enough to live somewhere with any sort of nature available within walking distance, I highly recommend taking advantage of it). Stillness exists within you. I used to go into the bathroom, lock the door behind me, and let water run in the sink to drown out noise outside the door. I'd stay there for maybe 10 minutes, just lying on the floor and breathing. It was the only time I could have some moments to myself without a child, pet, or husband needing something from me.

Find your stillness. It'll change your life.

Practice Gratitude

I know, I know. This sounds schmaltzy and false. You're thinking, *The world sucks! People are assholes! My life is freakin' impossible!*

I didn't know how to practice gratitude for the longest time. I honestly didn't believe there was anything to be grateful for. I was married to an emotionally abusive man. We had no money. I was miserable at my job. I genuinely believed I had nothing to offer the world. I could see no hopeful future, no way my life could ever be anything other than what it was — depressing drudgery for the entirety of existence.

But here's the thing. There's always something to be grateful for. Always. And it's worth spending just a few moments a day seeking it out and naming it.

At first it was little things, and I had to hunt for them. *My body and mind are sound. The sun is shining today. My daughter laughed, and it made me laugh too. I have a job. I have a roof over my head. We have food.* These things are easy to take for granted but not everyone in the world is fortunate enough to have them. Once I got in the habit of recognizing just exactly how fortunate I was, it became more difficult to complain about things I thought I didn't have.

Over time, the unexpected result was that I genuinely had less to complain about because, as I was focusing on things, people, and experiences present in my life I was grateful for, I began seeking out more of them, becoming less interested in remaining rooted in lack, jealousy, and low energy. I saw more of what I could be grateful for in my present life. And I desired to create even more opportunities to be so.

Try it for yourself, right now. Put this book aside for just a few moments. Recall one thing you feel gratitude for.

Perhaps it's the fact you have time to sit still and read this book. Maybe it's your day off, or your child is napping. Maybe the rain has stopped, or maybe it's started. Perhaps you have one friend you know you can turn to in times of need or have enough food in the refrigerator to create a meal for yourself or your family. There's nothing off-limits here, and there *is* something in your life you can raise up in gratitude.

If you feel stuck, because things right now seem to be pure and genuine shit, then I invite you to consider the following: Why choose that belief? Why remain committed to the idea there's no good present in your life? What's the payoff you receive for this false belief?

Do you get attention or sympathy for airing your griefs and tribulations? Are you afraid you might have to change if you start seeing your life differently? And if that's the case, can you breathe, feel your body, and invite the question: When did I start being afraid of being happy?

Being grateful doesn't equate being content with where we are, if where we are isn't fulfilling and healthy for our soul. Finding something to be grateful for doesn't mean there isn't difficulty in our life, that we're not hurting in a way that's all-consuming, or that everything will magically get better overnight. Gratitude isn't a panacea. But choosing to be grateful for seemingly small things will open the door for more things to be grateful for to appear. It will lighten your load while you carry your burdens. Gratitude is an invitation for more grace, light, and all that's good, holy, and beautiful to be made present in your world.

What do you have to lose except, perhaps, some negativity?

Be Tireless in Your Pursuit of Other's Goodness

It's so easy to judge and label other human beings. It's rewarding to our Ego to create stories about them and then believe in them wholeheartedly and without revision for eternity, no matter how many contrary pieces of evidence may show up to refute our narrative.

Of course, sometimes the opposite happens. Sometimes, someone really is nothing more than they appear to be, and their words and actions demonstrate who that is, repeatedly, and nothing occurs that *should* change our minds or hearts about them. These aren't the people we need to tirelessly pursue in our quest to find goodness in others.

The people I'm talking about are the ones someone else told us we shouldn't like, because for whatever reason (and they love to give us lots of reasons) *they* don't like them, and obviously their opinion is well-informed and sacred, and our opinion should fall in line with theirs.

Like the ones portrayed in a certain light in the movies and television shows we view, magazines we consume, advertising we're subjected to every way we turn, and news stories we watch and read.

They're the seemingly never-ending stream of brown skinned human beings leaving poverty-and-violence-stricken hometowns to make their dangerous way north to America for a chance at a life that isn't lived in perpetual fear who are painted as lazy, worthless, non-English speaking denigrates who swarm our borders, bringing with them crime and disease, who steal our jobs and live off us good, legal taxpayers.

Or perhaps they're rich, White, and conservative, so we automatically label them as selfish, greedy, racist, and out-of-touch with "reality" (our egoic version of it, of course.)

Maybe they wear head coverings or hairstyles that frighten us because we don't know what they mean. They look different, talk and dress differently, have different values than us, different religions than us, go to the wrong church or don't go to church at all, voted for the wrong person, or believe in the wrong things.

We need to meet these people. We need to ask them what their hopes, dreams, and fears are. We need to share with them ours. We need to break bread together and understand their journeys and we can't do that until we understand our own.

Why wouldn't we want to help give a better life to our fellow humans? Why are we so dismissive and judgmental of views that aren't our own? Why are we afraid of people who wear hijabs or Afros or straight, glossy blond locks?

Ask yourself these types of questions, relentlessly. Life presents us myriad opportunities to explore the goodness in ourselves and others. Why refuse that gift?

The Fifth Practice: Elevate the Good

If you're starting your day with this chapter, resolve right now to pay attention to the goodness running rampant in your world. When you witness a teenager looking up from their phone to laugh with their parents, or a parent looking up from their phone to answer their child's question, or you look up from your own phone to notice a flock of birds dancing synchronously across the arc of the sun — these are all moments worth elevating in your consciousness.

If you're reading this chapter at the close of your day, recall at least one good, holy, beautiful interaction you had with another human being. Perhaps the barista at your local coffee shop genuinely listened when you responded honestly to his requisite "How're you doing?" Perhaps a driver on the freeway graciously backed off so you could merge instead of speeding ahead to crowd you out. Recall something. Elevate it and give thanks for it.

Create more of what you seek in the world by finding, elevating, and demonstrating the grace and beauty it already houses.

Be tireless in your pursuit to see the good — the humanity — in others. Underneath all our differences, the things we have in common are that we love, and we fear. We want the best for ourselves and our loved ones. We want safety and security; nourishment in body, mind, and soul; and companionship. We're afraid of having these things stripped from us, or we're afraid we'll never have them at all.

We're not so different, you and I. Keep this truth close to your heart as you delve into the next chapter, where we focus on the very real, very ugly reality of racism, prejudice, bias, and privilege. Remember what we've learned about the importance of breath: this will be an excellent opportunity to practice.

7
Recognize Racism, Biases, and Prejudices

We Have Them. Let's Own Them, and Choose Anew.

Are you breathing? Good. Let's commit to working through this chapter together with grace for ourselves and others. Remember, anytime you feel that telltale rigidity creeping into your shoulders, jaw, or mind, stop. Set the book aside. Breathe. And come back when you once again feel ready to consider the words.

Let's pause for a moment and recall what Ego is (a self-created voice we've believed to be our best friend whom we know now is anything but) and what Ego does (keeps us locked in thoughts of fear, shame, doubt, and defensiveness). If we remember Ego's objective — to be "right" at all costs — perhaps we'll more easily recognize some of its most pervasive traps before they're sprung. Those traps often look like denial, deflection, and dismissiveness when it comes to challenging what we believe is true about race, gender, sexuality, or any other identity that feels fixed and natural.

Let's start by remembering racial violence didn't only happen decades or centuries ago; many iterations are occurring right now, across the globe. Our reptilian brains seem to be kicking into survival-mode overdrive as demographics change and societies shift; those mammalian instincts drive us to want to divide and conquer rather than unify and liberate.

Let's next be open to new ideas of what gender, sexuality, parenting, and all manner of relationships can and do look like. Let's commit to reminding ourselves that what works for us in our own lives may not work for others in theirs. And just as we want to feel free to make our own life choices and have those choices honored and respected, so, too, does everyone else.

We humans have a collective past many of us aren't proud of, a past many still refuse to reconcile with the social divides we're currently living with. But isn't erasing the ugly parts of our history and refusing to deal with its relevance today a denial of truth? And if we deny truth, aren't we denying ourselves the opportunity to fix what is so clearly broken? After all, if a system only benefits a relative few, can we honestly say that system works?

In the spirit of wanting to be an Authentically Good Human, can we acknowledge the painful past and ugly present of which we're *all* co-contributing members? Can we choose to come together with generosity of spirit, genuine curiosity for other's stories, and willingness to engage with people who don't think, look, act, talk, or believe like we do? Can we choose love for our fellow humans over fear of them?

Let's find out, together.

The Truth About Racism

In primitive times, it was useful to recognize when the creature ambling toward us was, say, a sabretooth tiger and not, in fact, a human; this burgeoning self-awareness kept us alive. But we've let those primitive instincts for tribal recognition (which are still very much part of our human DNA) run amok. We've divided ourselves into self-made categories based on physical attributes (like skin color) and geographical attributes (like where on the planet we were born) and then assigned meaning and value to those attributes. Those meanings and values are constructed in the society in which we live, inevitably by the dominate power structures (which get to create and enforce laws). And once those structures are erected, it's almost impossible to tear them back down.

It's important to have a common understanding of what racism *isn't*, so that we can talk intelligently with one another about what it *is*. Racism isn't simply individual bias or prejudice. Those are personal inclinations, (mis)understandings, ignorant judgments, and presumptions we *all* make about others based on everything from the language people speak, to their style of dress, to yes, the color of their skin. These presumptions, in and of themselves, may not necessarily generate harm — although they can, if left unchallenged.

Institutionalized racism takes those individual biases and prejudices and cements them into laws and policies (written and unwritten) that continually favor one group of human beings over another. While it's true individuals can and do hold racist beliefs, it's also true that not everyone can act upon their racism writ large, for one very simple reason: Institutionalized racism is personal prejudice *plus power.*

Who holds power in the society in which you live? How has that power manifested itself, historically? How is it manifesting today?

In America, racism was literally woven into the fabric of our country when we awarded personal and collective rights to human beings but then legally wrote all people of color out of the human family, thereby negating our responsibility to honor those rights. It's a contradiction we haven't yet fully addressed, or remedied.

I want to pause here. This is a time when many of my fellow White-identifying people feel angry and defensive. We think, *I've **never** condoned racism. My company has hired dozens of people of color. I have Black friends. People of color are racist, too.* All these things may be true. But consider the following story.

I recently participated in an antiracism workshop. We'd been asked to pair up and share a time we'd misjudged someone based solely on appearance. My partner, a self-identified Black woman, said she'd been approached by a White woman after giving a presentation and immediately brushed off her questions, assuming she wouldn't ask or share anything relevant. Later, she'd learned the woman she'd refused to engage with was a light skinned woman of color.

She said she regretted missing the opportunity to engage with another scholar who was also a woman of color; she didn't say anything about feeling badly for dismissing someone simply because the color of their skin appeared White.

It hurt to hear out loud such blatant disregard for the color of my own skin. It made me feel I, too, was being dismissed because of it. But instead of feeling angry, I felt sadness; this woman's beliefs had also kept *us* from sharing real dialogue and connection. She'd decided the color of my skin meant I had nothing of value to offer her.

And I found myself reflecting on how often, and for how long, White people have made people of color in my country feel the same way.

The experience, although painful, doesn't mean I don't need to consider and challenge the entrenched beliefs and practices that inform the social and political power structures in America today. It *does* mean we all have some work to do when it comes to untangling the personal and cultural influences that shape our understanding of our world.

After all, while we no longer see blatantly racist or discriminatory language dividing White people and people of color into segregated lines for bathrooms and bus stations, we do have legally backed social practices that disproportionately affect the life chances of Black and brown-skinned people negatively, especially when compared to Whites: People of color consistently rank lower than Whites in overall health, wealth, jobs, and educational opportunities while being incarcerated at 2½ to 6 times the rate of White people. What if those numbers aren't reflective of individual abilities or choices but are instead emblematic of larger, institutional problems?

What I mean by life chances are the things that make life worth living, and which allow us to do so with a modicum of comfort and security. I mean easy access to fresh, affordable whole food, not just fast-food junk. I mean parks with green trees and swaths of grass within walking distance of our neighborhoods, no matter how far into the city we might live. I mean the ability to see a doctor whenever we need them, which means we have transportation to do so and won't be turned away because we can't pay.

I mean the privileges many of us reading this book may never have to stop and think about.

Real Privilege and False Guilt

Privilege. It's a word that's everywhere these days, and so triggering to some people that they immediately get angry, tune out, and miss out on an incredibly rich opportunity to dialogue with themselves about their fears, presumptions, and assumptions. (I know, I know. Not everyone finds this fun. It genuinely baffles me).

Time for some self-inquiry. Grab a pen and notepad and come back when you're ready.

Got it? Good. Now take a few moments to jot down the ideas that come to mind when I ask this question:

What five words would you use to describe the most important aspects of your identity?

We naturally tend to list things that have impacted us the most in our life experiences, the things that helped shape and define the person we believe ourselves to be. For me, the list looks a little something like this: Woman. Mother. Wife. Daughter. Writer.

My identity, first, is as a woman. This identifier has personally shaped my life in ways quite different from my husband, son, or father. In fact, when my husband did this exercise, he didn't even list the identifier "man" or "male." Instead, everything revolved around the roles he plays: husband, stepdad, son, IT guy, outdoor enthusiast. He's never stopped to think about his gender as an identifier; perhaps he's never needed to. My life, however, has been inarguably shaped by being a woman.

This list might look quite different for people who identify as anything other than cis-gendered (for those who'd like a primer, this simply means the gender you identify with and outwardly express matches the biological sex you were assigned at birth). How would my identifiers read if I'd lived a life wherein I wasn't allowed to express my gender or sexuality in a way that felt safe and supported? I'm guessing those labels would quickly become incredibly salient to how I describe myself to others. Instead, I've never had to think about it.

That is privilege.

I've been *privileged* to move through life rather easily, in the sense that my gendered appearance and my sexual orientation match the normative same-sex preferences our society's prescribed. I've never been singled out for transgressing those particular unwritten social rules. Nor have I had to consciously think about the color of my skin because as a middle-class White woman, I can do things like drive with a broken taillight, walk in my neighborhood at night, raise my voice to people who're treating me unfairly, and browse a store's offerings without purchasing anything without worrying about being targeted, harassed, potentially arrested, or harmed.

Privilege.

The first time I did the identifier exercise, I was shocked, then dismayed, and then ashamed that I never realized what a privilege it was to move through the world in a way that never had me questioning the color of my skin, my gender expression, or my sexuality. And do you know why I've never had to think about it? Because America, especially, is set up for my success as a straight, heteronormative White person. Our society has normalized this particular set of identities and set them as the ideal to attain, even offering incentives for being so: For example, we created laws that rewarded opposite-sex marriage with tax breaks while denying that same benefit to couples who were the same sex.

Privilege.

It doesn't mean I haven't struggled. It doesn't mean I'm not still struggling. It simply means my life chances are exponentially better than many people of color and LGBTQIA+ people in the world — not because I've necessarily earned it, deserve it, or have worked harder for it. It's partly because the color of my skin, the presentation of my gender, and my sexuality all fall comfortably within the norms of my American society.

We don't need to feel guilt at what has come to pass; guilt tends to keep us too stuck to move. Nor do we need to deny our achievements; accepting the truth of our relative privilege doesn't negate our hard work. But can we choose to take ownership over what currently exists? Can we ponder the idea that those of us who identify as White and straight might operate from a privileged position? Can we be willing to use that privilege as an asset to elevate the voices and experiences of those who've been silenced for so long? Or will we choose to remain blissfully ignorant of our privilege and relative power and refuse to do anything to change the tide or break the norms? Will we continually refuse to stand up, stand out, and help burn it all to the ground (metaphorically, of course!) so something more equitable and just can rise in its place?

I, as a straight White woman, have that privilege of choice. Many people who fall outside traditional ideas of acceptability don't: couples who are the same sex; individuals who dress, behave, and identify as a gender other than the one assigned them at birth; and families consisting of something other than one male father and one female mother who are married and live under the same roof.

Here, dear reader, I pose some questions to ponder: Is it possible to allow what I've written to be true, even if it goes against what you've always believed about race, gender, or sexuality? Can we be gentle with one another as we struggle together with these shifting definitions? Can we gracefully acknowledge the very real fears of our brothers and sisters who might be watching their entire Ego world crumble? Can we maintain faith they'll *want* to come alongside us if only we extend a hand, rather than forcing theirs?

What Are We Afraid of, Really?

What do we get to hold onto if we refuse to let go of our beliefs? There's always a payoff, a reward of some kind. The reward may be totally imagined, and it most likely won't be something that serves us (after all, if we're resisting something that strongly, it's most likely our Ego back in charge, and we've already agreed that little bugger isn't our best friend).

If we refuse to name racism, sexism, or any other "ism" in America — refuse to look squarely in their institutional-and-law-supported eyes — what we get to hold onto is our privilege and power. We get to remain comfortable. We get to say it's not our fault, whatever *it* may be. We get something out of it. And on the path to becoming a Good Human, it's our job to figure out what.

Welcome to the work. Continue to breathe.

The Sixth Practice: Immerse

As you've read these words, what's popped up for you? Are you nodding along in agreement, breezing through with no hesitation? Are you slamming the book shut and hurling it across the room in anger? Are you only mildly annoyed, wondering why I must bring race, gender, and sexuality into it at all? All of these are valid responses.

Here's what I invite you to do, no matter how you respond to the ideas I've proposed here: Read the following instructions, then put the book down.

Take a deep belly breath, then another, and then one more. Take note of where you're feeling sensations in your body.

Name them. Don't get attached to them; just witness. Then, when you feel centered, ask yourself these questions:

- What do I believe about race?
- When did I first start believing these things about race?
- Who was the first person, or what was the first event, that introduced me to the concept of race?
- What do my parents/children/friends/church congregation/coworkers/social circles believe about race? Do I agree or disagree with those beliefs? Why?
- What am I willing to admit I don't understand about race?

We can use this same set of questions for any belief system that's uncomfortable for us to question. For example, try replacing "race" with "gender," "sexuality," or "religion" and see what comes up for you.

Remember to keep breathing and checking in with your body as you respond to these questions. If you notice you've stopped breathing from the belly; if your belly, throat, jaw, or eyes are tight; or if your mind wanders away from the questions, these are good signs you're feeling resistance to something I've written. It's a beautiful time to discover what, and why.

※

However you identify, I hope this chapter has allowed you to question some of your own belief systems surrounding ideas of race, gender, sexuality, or anything else that feels sticky for you. On the path to becoming a Good Human, I don't think anyone gets a pass on challenging themselves to outgrow ideologies that don't allow the full expression of humanity.

In the next chapter, we'll recall what it means to be truly empathetic, to remember the humanity housed within the sometimes-rigid bodies of our fellow human beings, and learn how to be brave enough to stand up when everyone else remains sitting down.

8
Weep When Others Weep
Become Adept at Being an Empath

We've talked about looking for goodness in others. But it isn't enough to acknowledge *Yes, okay, this person has some traits that maybe aren't terrible all the time.* It's too easy in heated moments to forget their goodness — their humanity — if all we've done is surface-level excavation. We need to keep digging to truly see and then *name* the goodness we find so we can easily recall it in the toughest moments, the ones when we're challenged by our egoic habits and inclinations to forget.

When we remember the body in front of us speaking words that scare or enrage us is also nothing more and nothing less than an equally flawed human being, we allow ourselves the space to return to our Authenticity. We give ourselves a moment to breathe instead of lashing out or reacting; we create room for genuinely curious questions to arise instead of attacks.

Seek out the humanity in others. Offer them the chance to find yours.

This Human is Your Equal

I'm going to clue you in on a little secret that will have you skyrocketing to first place in the race to be the very best Good Human: You and I are no better than any other human being on this planet. Not one. Not now, not in the future. Not ever.

It doesn't matter how much money we have in the bank. It doesn't matter the list of accolades, awards, praise, and positive reviews we might want to show off. It doesn't matter how many self-help books we've read and spiritual retreats we've attended. It doesn't matter the zip code in which we live, the church we attend, how we spend our time and money, how many followers we have on Instagram, YouTube, Twitter, or TikTok, or how big our retirement portfolio is.

None of these things make us amazing or even very special. We're still no better than the houseless people sleeping on the street, the addict spending their money on their next high, the parent neglecting their child, or the brown-skinned person crossing an invisible line onto land we think we have a right to possess just because we were born on it. And here's why.

At some point in our life, we've been a terrible human being. We've done and said things that wounded others. We've been selfish. We felt hatred for someone. We hurt someone we said we loved. We were lazy, unkind, skipped work, ran out of money, refused to give our child the attention they craved, lied to our spouse, used a derogatory term to describe another human, drank too much, flipped off another driver, or made excuses as to why we couldn't possibly accomplish this, that, or the other thing.

We're human, which means we're flawed. We've failed, which means we're perfectly poised to have compassion for other human beings when they inevitably fail, too. After all, we didn't get to where we are without help: We may have pulled ourselves up by our bootstraps but first someone bought us the damn boots, put them on our feet, and showed us how to tie the freakin' laces. No one is born knowing it all — someone had to teach us. To claim otherwise is simply false.

So, let's stop pretending we earned it all by ourselves and therefore everyone else can and should, too. We didn't. They can't. Full stop. Let's reach out a hand and help someone stand. Just as someone, somewhere, once did for us.

We Have More in Common Than We Want to Admit

Do you know what Republicans want? Money in their pockets and for their values to be heard and respected. Do you know what Democrats want? The exact same freakin' thing. Independents? Same. You? Check. Me? Yup.

I'm going to be bold and controversial here and go so far as to say that Evangelical Christians, Muslim fundamentalists, far-right extremists, and members of Antifa probably also want the same things. (Bear with me before you take to social media to accuse me of being a supporter of the Proud Boys or Antifa. It's emphatically untrue).

We're human beings. We all love, and we all fear. We want ourselves and our loved ones healthy, happy, and whole. We celebrate wins and mourn losses. We get stuck, and then unstuck, and then stuck again. Some of us are farther along the path toward destination Love and Freedom than others, but we've all gotten mired in the muck of hatred and fear at some point along that path. We have these things in common.

If you've stuck with me to this point, you know I believe that goodness in human beings stems from a few fundamental concepts: We breathe and tune into our bodies to discover what we already know but don't want to admit. We relentlessly question our beliefs and ideologies. We fearlessly ask others about theirs with genuine curiosity and without judgment. We listen. We engage. And we allow ourselves to have our minds changed if that means releasing toxicity from our lives and elevating our goodness *and* the goodness of other humans.

For that to be true, it means I must acknowledge that everyone's journey is different; in each of those differing journeys, I must allow others to be where they are, accept their level of stuckness or freedom, bless them on their route, and refocus on mine.

It doesn't mean I agree with them. It doesn't mean I condone ideologies of hate, fear, and violence, or that I don't do anything to counteract hateful rhetoric or actions. Just because I can see the egoic fear monsters running someone and understand how easy it is for them to let that little voice remain their best friend, doesn't mean I excuse the things they say that are blatantly racist, purposefully harmful, or patently untrue. It simply means I recognize them as a fellow human being who is choosing to walk a certain path.

Theirs is not a path I choose to walk. And I'm much more interested in helping other, willing humans discover alternative paths than I am in following certain people down theirs, trying to make them turn around and see the other routes available.

Why not leave those alternative paths free for humans willing to venture forward into new territories, who aren't threatened by what may be around the bend but who are instead excited to find out?

Discover What You Don't Know ('Cause You Don't Know Anything)

Ah. Another basic truth that's so difficult for us humans to admit: We don't know anything about anyone. I mean, we hardly even know ourselves. Why are we so certain we can know others?

We see someone and think we have them all figured out: Teenage mom? Promiscuous. A brown-skinned person speaking Spanish? Illegal immigrant. Houseless person on the street? Drug addict. White person flying an American flag on the back of their motorcycle? White supremacist.

C'mon. These are all childish labels we assign to other human beings based on nothing more than a glimpse. Ego convinces us those glimpses tell us everything we need to know, and we don't bother to ask or learn anything more. For instance, in every single one of those examples, if we were to bother taking the time to pause and ask ourselves, *Why do I think that?* what might happen? To start, we might realize the reason we came up with those labels is because the media and our own social groups provided them for us; we didn't even think of them ourselves. We just took what was given us as "fact" and applied it to another human, or group of humans, without a second thought.

Yikes. I hate to think what other people might automatically assume about me if they saw me for the first time at the grocery store at noon, after I've been up for five hours writing furiously, forgetting to change out of my sweats or brush my hair before going out in public. Probably that I'm a lazy, good-for-nothing jobless woman with nothing important going on in my life who doesn't care about her appearance. (To be fair, that last part is true. I don't care about my appearance. If *you* care about my appearance, you're bound to be disappointed).

What this example illustrates is that you can't know by looking at me in my stained sweatpants, tangled hair, and socks-with-Crocs that I'm feverishly pursuing a lifelong dream that doesn't allow such vanity projects as taking a shower or brushing my teeth; that I live in a lovely house with an attic room that streams light upon my antique writing desk; and that I have a husband, son, and adorably needy rescue pup at home, all of whom are anxiously awaiting my return with snacks and drinks for an impromptu picnic outside on our shade-strewn deck. I'm working hard for my loving family.

But even if I weren't — even if I *were* that "good-for-nothing, lazy woman…" Well, guess what? I *have* been her. I lived her for most of my life. And when I was her, I was *still* deserving of your empathy, *never* of your judgment.

We can't know what life is like for that young mother, Spanish-speaking person, or houseless person. We can't know the ideas and ideals that motivate someone to proudly wave their country's flag. That is, we can't know if we don't ask. And if we don't want to bother inquiring, then we really don't have the right to spend time and energy concocting stories about human beings that do nothing more than inflate our egoic sense of superiority.

We can remember this core truth: We're not better than any other human being, no matter their story.

If we do ask, and it turns out that young woman had dozens of sexual partners before she became pregnant; if that Spanish-speaking person *is* crossing the border "illegally" dozens of times a year; if that person living in a tent next to our neighborhood park is a heroin addict with no intention of quitting; and if the White person with the American flag confirms their belief in White superiority, we can remind ourselves that these are their journeys. We can ask ourselves the following to return to a state of empathy rather than judgment:

What must it be like to be a sexually awakened young woman in a society that tells her that her only worth is how attractive she is to men and boys, one in which there's no easy or affordable access to reproductive and sexual healthcare? What would cause people to travel far from home in search of low-paying work (by my middle-class American standards), and to keep doing it even after they've been arrested and deported? How terrifying must it be for that addict to not know where they're going to sleep every night or if they're going to find food? What fears and limiting beliefs might be running rampant in a person espousing ideas of White supremacy ?

These are the questions we ask. We remember we don't know, and that even if they tell us some of their story, we still won't know it all because rarely do we show ourselves fully to another human being, especially when we feel vulnerable. Especially when we're in pain.

Humankind is in pain right now. Every time we hurl an accusation or epithet at another human being or that human being's ideas, we're piercing our own skin with yet another layer of fear and loathing. We're furthering our divisions rather than forging the connections that come when we remember our own defeats and choose to extend grace and empathy, rather than judgment and fear.

The Seventh Practice: Cultivate Empathy

It takes bravery to become genuinely curious about our thoughts, beliefs, and ideologies, especially if we run in social circles that reward us for remaining true to stereotypes and stories already propagated about other individuals and groups of human beings.

Go back and reread the examples I provided regarding the young mother; Spanish-speaking, brown-skinned person; houseless person; and American flag-toting White person. What stereotypical labels did I assign each one?

If you remember, I equated a teenage mother with promiscuity; a brown-skinned person speaking Spanish as an illegal immigrant; a houseless person as a drug addict; and a White person with an American flag as a White supremacist. Did you find yourself picturing these people and understanding why those particular labels were applied? Or did you feel confused as to why they were included, unable to relate at all to the picture I was painting? What do my examples tell you about my own journey and judgments? Well, I was able to come up with those examples and labels so easily because they're ones I've seen, heard, and repeated in my own life.

What does your reaction to these examples tell you about your own journey and judgments? What don't you know about the human beings you encounter in your daily life? What don't your peers know about the human beings they see portrayed in movies, books, and news?

Are we willing to find out? Are we brave enough to require the people we spend time with to find out along with us?

Reflecting on these questions is how we create empathy. Acting on them is how we forge connections. This is what it takes to become a truly Good Human.

※

Seek the humanity in other human beings. Weep when they weep, without judgment, and without needing to fix them. Let them see your tears and know you cry with them. Be willing to show them a more Authentic way of being and let go any need to control their choices. Love them even as they hate or self-destruct. This is empathy: a willingness to walk a mile in someone else's shoes to feel a glimmer of the inner landscapes they inhabit.

Feel their pain. See their fear. Acknowledge your own. When, in your own life, have you made mistakes, been afraid, cowered or raged, let something other than your Authentic Self guide you? Often, right? It's what led you to pick up this book and probably several more like it. Be empathetic, especially to the human beings your Ego thinks are least deserving.

Allow your fellow human beings their journey. Be thankful you're allowed your own. Remember this guidance as we dive deep into the stickiness of ideological belief systems in the next chapter.

Part III: The Arrival

9
Interrogate Your Beliefs
Believe in Something Bigger Than Yourself,
Your Ideologies, and Your Idols

We all live by a set of values and beliefs we hope will guide us on our complicated journeys through life. Rarely are they examined, but they absolutely need to be, as these values and beliefs are inevitably learned and inherited from others. In and of themselves, they're neither positive nor negative — they simply exist because we created them (or, had them created for us). Problems arise when we start believing we *are* our values and beliefs: If someone disagrees with them, we think they're attacking us. When we feel attacked, we defend at all costs. What are we really defending?

If we're operating from Ego mind, what we're defending is the invented picture of ourselves we've been carrying around since childhood, one bequeathed to us by our parents, caretakers, teachers, and friends. Ego needs us to remain attached to those values and beliefs we've come to know so well because without them, it thinks we'll have no worth or importance. Our Authentic Selves, however, don't have anything to defend against; even when someone disagrees with our values and beliefs, we remain open, free of judgment, and trusting.

What if we could take a step back from the belief systems we so often desperately identify with, see them as nothing more than thoughts we've had, and admit because they're nothing but thoughts they can be changed? We don't *have* to change them, obviously, but admitting we *could* is one giant step forward on our path to becoming and remaining a Good Human.

Mired in the Muck of Ideology

I want to tease out the difference between values, beliefs, and ideologies. Values tend to inform our beliefs, which form the bedrock of our ideologies. If our value system changes, then our belief system tends to follow suit, as does our ideology. But if our values remain steadfast, it becomes harder to see how our beliefs surrounding those values can shift. If our beliefs can't shift, that means they're rigid; if they're rigid, then our ideologies will remain mired in muck.

Some of my core values — the things that make up Authentic Me, the things that haven't shifted, the things that give me the foundation upon which I build my house — are integrity, honesty, commitment to equality and justice, and growth. These are the principles I live by. I don't feel good in my body, mind, or spirit when I veer from any of these values: My body becomes sluggish, my thoughts turn defensive, and my tone gets harsh when I haven't told the whole truth or failed to meet a commitment.

What this means is that I have a difficult time not telling the truth, even if that truth makes me "look bad"; I get all kinds of fired up when I read or hear about human beings treated in inhumane ways; and I try not to stay married to my opinions because on a journey of growth, I simply can't do that — the two ideas (growth and stagnation) are diametrically opposed.

Think of your own value system. What comes to mind when you think of the things that are important to Authentic You? Remember, these aren't things your Ego tells you that you *should* value. These are the things that sustain you when everything else fades away.

Do you value freedom? Democracy? Law and order? Hard work? Kindness? Friendship? Harmony? The list of values we subscribe to is endless and, again, there are no right or wrong answers. Once you've nailed down even a few values think next about the belief systems you carry that mirror those values.

For example, because I *value* equality and justice, I advocate for things like a reduction in police and military forces, a shift in spending from those services to things like community policing and mental health services, and antiracism training for all public service sectors. I *believe* these methods will work to reduce the number of caged human bodies — especially brown and Black ones. But these beliefs are just that: ideas I choose to believe in because they're in alignment with my values. As much as I believe in them, I must also be willing to let them go.

It can feel infuriating to move through the world with human beings who don't live by the same values we hold. That is, it feels infuriating if we believe our fellow human beings *must* live by the values we hold but they refuse to do so. That "must" is Ego desperation: It's the very cause of such infuriation and exact opposite of operating from Authenticity.

It was incredibly painful for me to learn as a child that not everyone around me valued truth-telling and integrity the way I did. It came as a genuine shock to learn through experience that people — adults, even! — could look me in the face and lie, or that their behavior didn't exactly line up with what they preached in church on Sundays. I automatically assumed every human being I encountered carried the same value system I did, which meant being dishonest would hurt them the same way it hurt me and they'd never consider doing it.

My confusion and consequential anger were nothing more than a result of my own misguided and uninformed expectation that everyone needed to live by my rules; it wasn't because of other people's behavior. As I grew, I learned how easy it is to lie, to not live in integrity, and to speak lofty words you then immediately turn around to contradict with your actions. We see this in politics every single day. We see it in religion every single day. We see it in parenting, educational institutions, police departments, and government. It's something unfortunately very common: Not everyone lives by the values they profess to carry, which makes it even more confounding to determine why some people remain so outwardly committed to their belief systems when they act in direct opposition to the values they profess to cherish.

If we're paying attention to the words and actions of others, we can pretty easily detect when the two are incongruous with each other or out of alignment with their professed values. First, though, we must be willing to detect it within ourselves.

It always comes back to us. We are who we're responsible for, just as every other human being is equally responsible for themselves.

Allow Others Their Beliefs — Even When They're "Wrong"

My spirituality revolves around the mystical teachings of Jeshua ben Joseph (Western Christianity's Jesus) as channeled through various entities. Jeshua asks a question I return to often when I realize I'm rigidly clinging to my beliefs and ideologies, lashing out in anger at people who don't live by them, and feeling righteous indignation at the state of affairs in the world: *What would you seek to control except that which you distrust?*

Let me ask that again:

What would you seek to control *except* that which you distrust?

I sometimes distrust my own ability to live steadfastly by my proclaimed values. After all, can I say with utmost honesty that I *always* tell unadulterated truth? Nope. Do I sometimes laze about in self-pity and fear instead of choosing the path of radical growth? Of course I do. As I prove to myself time and again, I also fall into the trap of Ego consciousness more often than I care to admit.

We all have entire lists of people whom we think are inherently "wrong" about pretty much everything in life. For some of us, it's those who oppose abortion; for others, those who support it. For some of us, it's those who create laws banning the teachings of antiracism; for others, those who bring it into our children's classrooms. And for some of us, it's those who refuse to wear masks and get vaccinated during a worldwide pandemic while for others, it's those who mandate that we must.

We don't think we're wrong in these beliefs. We don't *think* we're wrong, which implies we *think* we're right. What is it that needs to be "right" in all these situations?

Ego will defend our beliefs with every trick in its playbook – counterattack, judgment, hostility, and self-righteousness; after all, our beliefs align perfectly with the identities we often so fervently cling to.

Perhaps we distrust what might happen if, instead of stubbornly clinging to our idealistic positions, we reached out to ask genuinely curious questions of those with opposing viewpoints. Maybe we distrust the Authentic person we might become if we choose to hear what other people have to say and allow our egoic worlds to crumble. Or maybe, just maybe, what we distrust is our own ability to live our lives Authentically and meaningfully without needing others approval and agreement.

We can't control others' values and beliefs and we can't say definitively that our values and beliefs are better, more valuable, or more "right" than anyone else's.

What are you seeking to control? What is it you distrust? Exploring these two questions will yield a treasure trove of beliefs just waiting to be unearthed.

Abide in Abundance Instead of Lack

I want to preface this section with a disclaimer.

We live in a vastly inequitable society. There are human beings who genuinely do live in lack, who are forced to operate from a place of scarcity because of things like generational poverty, lack of access to affordable healthcare, anything even resembling a decent education, job training, jobs that pay an actual living wage, and affordable childcare (even if those living-wage jobs did exist).

This section isn't about those humans. This section is for those of us fortunate enough to not have to worry about how to put a meal on the table in front of ourselves or our families; who can afford to own a car or two and the gas to put in them; and who have more than we need to live a good, healthy, and productive life.

We're behaving as if we need more, like we don't have enough. Like someone is going to come snatch what we do have from us if we let "them" come over the "border" or give "them" dreaded "welfare." (I put quotes around "border" and "welfare" because they're both terms we humans arbitrarily assigned to concepts we invented: These terms were created by human thought. We've all agreed to use them in specific ways and those ways tend to take on negative connotations because our society tells us this is so).

This is what it boils down to: When we're in Ego we're operating from a place of lack and fear. We think our resources are scarce; that what we need to survive is limited and, therefore, needs to be protected at all costs; and that getting ourselves more of those resources is worth giving up our own inner joy and peace. But this is simply untrue. Everything we need to survive is readily available to all human beings, no matter how many of us live on the planet at any given time.

Pause, take a breath, and reread that.

Everything we need to survive is readily available to *all* human beings.

I'm not talking about finite resources. What I mean when I talk about what we need to survive is something different: the inner stuff no one can take away from us. The things inside that would allow us to face actual resource scarcity with fortitude, grace, and an ability and desire to share provisions. The precious gifts of Authenticity we carry every moment of our existence: Love. Growth. Expansion.

If that sounds a little too woo-woo and feel-goody, consider this:

We've talked about gratitude. Take a moment to flip back a few pages and look at what you wrote down that you were grateful for. A sunny day? Your child's laughter? The fact you're alive and breathing? Well, guess what? No one can take those things away from you; if you're experiencing them, they exist.

When we think, feel, and behave from a place of real abundance instead of lack or scarcity, it becomes much easier to move through the world with courage rather than fear, to court more abundance rather than spend useless time in worry or angst attempting to control that which we distrust, to welcome more human beings into a circle of safety and light rather than banish them to poverty, violence, and darkness just because we're afraid of what they might take from us.

What if by welcoming other human beings with open arms — by sharing our abundance and fortune with them — we gained something? What if there's something they'd love to give us, too?

The Eighth Practice: Identify Values

Return to those values you landed on earlier in the chapter, or if you didn't spend any time there, do so now: Think of half a dozen values you feel are important that guide you through life. Remember, values are usually traits we admire in others or aspire to embody ourselves. Write down your values and spend a few moments breathing and reading them over to yourself.

Now, focus on just one of those values, one that resonates as a core value for you. Take a breath, and ask this question: *Why?* Why is it important for you to live your life according to this value? Let whatever arises develop fully into an answer. Don't try to force that answer or change what comes up. Just allow yourself to explore the answer to the question *why?*

Next, ask yourself, *What beliefs do I hold about this value?* Same thing: breathe and observe. Write down what's revealed.

Then, finish these statements, starting and ending with breath:

- If others *don't* share my values, then _____ will occur.
- If _____ occurs, I'm afraid _____ will happen.
- If others *do* share my values and beliefs, then _____ will occur.
- And if _____ occurs, I believe _____ will happen.

End by asking: Can I know with 100% certainty that either of these scenarios is true? (Hint: The answer is no.)

❦

We're inevitably going to stumble on the path to becoming a Good Human. It's difficult, at first, to release our commitment to the values, beliefs, and ideologies we've lived by, especially if we've allowed Ego to convince us they're good, wise, and worth holding onto. But it's never wise to plant our feet so firmly in the muck of our idols — the ideas and people we worship — that we can't take a step forward onto a new path or take a step back to look at and question where we've been.

In the next chapter, we'll practice what I've preached throughout this entire book and learn how to do something truly radical: Change our minds.

10
Let Your Mind Be Changed
The Divine Wisdom of *Kinky Boots*

Aside from featuring the insanely talented Chiwetel Ejiofor, the 2005 film *Kinky Boots* offers viewers a sage reminder that we have *no* chance of finding the humanity in others if we choose to remain rigidly attached to our stories about them, rather than becoming genuinely curious.

In the film, Ejiofor plays Lola, a popular drag queen. In the provincial town in which Lola works, there's a group of humans confused by and vociferously opposed to Lola's lifestyle choices, people who make their dislike of this lifestyle known with violent actions and words. One of these people is Don, a traditionally depicted White male who is slightly overweight, likes to look at and comment on women's bodies, and who, upon discovering Lola is a man, becomes angry, confrontational, and vindictive.

In one beautifully scripted scene, Don and Lola face off in an arm-wrestling contest. As the two sit opposite one another over a sticky bar table, we see Lola take a surreptitious look around herself. She notes the size of the crowd: friends and enemies alike gathered around, some silently begging her to win for all the queer folx out there, some loudly proclaiming her inevitable defeat.

Together with Lola, we realize winning this arm-wrestling contest means the world to Don — literally. The Ego world he's constructed, the people and ideologies he's gathered around himself means he can't lose this contest to a drag queen: his egoic world would shatter. The terror of this knowledge is clear in his eyes as he takes his place across from Lola.

As this realization dawns, we understand she's not going to win. Not because she can't, but because she doesn't need to; her world is not as fragile as Don's. There's nothing for her to prove.

After Lola's defeat, as Don's friends slap him on the back and jeer at the properly chastened drag queen who dared threaten their comfortable world, Lola and Don share a moment. He asks Lola why she so obviously let him win.

"Well, Don," she replies, "I wouldn't want you to have to walk into work and feel disrespected. No. I wouldn't want *anyone* to feel that." Here, she turns to look at him directly. "Would you?"

Before walking away, Lola slips Don a note and whispers, "Change your mind about somebody."

This is what we're going to do repeatedly on the path to being a Good Human. We're going to decide to change our mind about somebody. And we're going to trust those humans we've changed our minds about will turn around and do the exact same thing. In this way will we truly be the change we want to see in the world.

Change our minds, change the world. This is where the work takes root.

There Is No Us, There Is No Them

One of the easiest ways to cause division among human beings is to convince us we're different from others. In that difference lies a specialness, either ours or theirs: Either we're *way* more special than they are, or they're *way* more special than us.

Here's the thing: There's no such thing as "us" and there's no such thing as "them." The entire concept is just manufactured bullshit we've all come to adopt as natural, obvious, and understood.

There's nothing *natural* about this man-made division of humanity into caste systems. There's nothing *obvious* that says one group of individual humans should have more (or less) power and privilege in the world than any other group of individuals. There should be no *understanding* of the way we've ordered our societies into continuously warring factions.

There's one group of human beings on this planet: Homo sapiens. That's it. End of story.

Within our species live a wide and glorious variety of individuals made up of unique combinations of cells that express themselves in all sorts of different ways. Thank goodness! Can you imagine how freakin' boring it would be if we all looked, acted, talked, and walked the exact same way; if we all believed the same ideologies; if we all had the same experiences of living and so had nothing to share with one another that was tantalizing, eye-opening, life-giving, and scrumptious?

Yet this seems to be the homogenization so many people are calling for right now, in tones ever more vehement and violent. Why? What benefit could such homogenization bring to humanity? Turns out, quite a lot, *if* we're committed to living inauthentically from Ego, projecting onto others our fears and insecurities, and hoarding power and privilege for ourselves and our like-minded peers.

By introducing the concept of "other," the opposite — a sense of belonging — is inevitably born. On the surface, this seems perfectly benign: After all, don't we all want to feel we belong somewhere? But in asking this question we've forgotten we already *do* belong. We have a vast, almost incomprehensible human family spanning the entire globe. We simply haven't allowed ourselves to recognize them yet.

Remember, we have more in common than we want to admit. We yearn for love and connection, safety and empathy, respect, and to feel valued. Anyone who convinces you to forget that your fellow human beings are, well, *human*, is doing so for a very specific purpose, which is never benign. It's *always* selfish, designed to elevate their own positions of invented power while stomping to the ground people they deem less worthy. Allowing such division to manifest will never serve our Authentic selves. It'll never serve the world we're striving to create.

Leave the Cave

Plato's Cave. The famous allegory about human beings living in a cave, facing a wall full of odd, flickering shadows and light. No one ever turns from the wall until one day, someone does. And when they do, they see a mysterious thing: Other humans, decidedly *not* facing the wall, walking around the cave, causing those lights to flicker as they move back-and-forth in front of a fire. The newly enlightened sneak out of the cave, see and experience all sorts of mysterious and wonderful things, and can't wait to return to the cave to free those whom they now understand to be their fellow captives. But alas, upon arrival, their stories of life outside the cave are met with derision and scorn. They learn a bitter lesson: Not everyone *wants* to leave the cave. Why?

Let's think about this for a second. What does the cave give them? Warmth. Shelter. Security. A known entity. Someone else making all the hard decisions. No responsibility. No risk. No fear. What they can't understand, of course, is that they're also not experiencing all that comes along with fear, risk, and responsibility — namely love, growth, and freedom.

They're not living a human life. They're cowering in place and allowing others to do it for them.

My cave, for the longest time, was supported by walls of inability and worthlessness. I was absolutely committed to such thoughts as: *You can't do that — you're not good enough; You'll never make enough money to support the kids on your own, so you better stay married; Yes, that person is successful, but look how much smarter/more attractive/popular they are. You can't be that.*

Do you know what I got for all those years of defeatist thinking? I got to stay small. I never had to risk failure because I wasn't bothering to try anything. I got to stay "safe" because I wasn't the one who had to be out there making money to support the family. I got to play victim, which meant I didn't have to take responsibility for my anger, sadness, or the hurt I inflicted on those around me.

I got a lot out of being incapable and worthless. But once I turned around from the walls of my cave, I couldn't turn back. I tried for a long time to be just as content as I'd been before to sit and stare at shadows other people were making. But something restless inside didn't want to stay put any longer. So finally, I chose to leave my cave for good.

The same people are still in there staring at the same damn wall, knowing there's something better outside (because I and all who came before me told them), but still, there they sit, more committed to fear than to love, to safety than to risk, to security than to Self.

I implore you — leave the cave. Turn around from the wall you've been planted in front of to see what else and who else may be out there.

Admit It: You Were Wrong

If we've done some inner work, we can admit our thoughts are not our own; the voice in our head is not, in fact, our best friend; and we ourselves have at one time or another been down on our luck, needed a hand up, or just behaved stupidly. The next step is to accept having been wrong.

Remember, our beliefs are not *us*. They're simply thoughts we've become attached to for reasons our Ego thinks will serve us. Logically, then, when our beliefs turn out to be incorrect, it doesn't mean we — our Authentic Selves — are under attack, have lesser value, are stupid, or anything else negative we may want to believe about ourselves. It just means there was once a time we believed this thing. This thing turns out to be false or incorrect. So now we can let that belief go. And that's that.

Let's return to my cave for a moment. When I believed I was too worthless for anyone to care about, it seemed obvious that meant I couldn't forge relationships (because who would be interested?), which meant I couldn't make friends, apply for jobs paying anything above minimum wage, earn a college degree, or try for anything that would've propelled me forward into a more fulfilling life. But once I left my cave and accepted never returning, it became ridiculous to continue insisting I was somehow unlikeable, unhireable, and unteachable: I'd had too many experiences that proved my false thinking wrong. I became friends with coworkers. I was hired for higher-paying jobs with greater responsibilities. I aced all my newly enrolled college classes.

Problems occur when we get too rigidly attached to beliefs that crumble in the face of logic, reason, and facts. We refuse to acknowledge this proof of our incorrect thinking, instead clinging ever more tightly to it. We do this because we fear that giving up this belief would leave us rudderless, directionless, and perhaps friendless. After all, we've believed this for so long, and perhaps everyone around us believes it, and if we say out loud, "I was wrong," won't we implode from shame and self-loathing?

No. Not only will we not implode, but we'll actually get bigger, tougher, and more alive. A giant weight will be lifted from our shoulders and chest we didn't even realize we were carrying.

Now's a great time to take a little self-inventory. Are you carrying around a belief that's been proven false? If so, ask yourself why that is. Is there a payoff you get for continuing to believe the thought (for example, my lack of having to take responsibility as long as I felt properly victimized by the world)?

Ask yourself: "Is this thought or belief *true*? How can I know that for sure? Do I have any evidence suggesting otherwise?"

Would You Rather Be Right or Happy?

For the longest time, I was committed to being right, and I was decidedly *not* happy. I was so sure I was right about everything: how people felt about me, how I felt about myself, and how I viewed the world and all the human beings moving through it. I was convinced everyone was living a much more fulfilling/fun/productive/successful life than me, that everyone was happier than me, and that my "instincts" about people and situations were correct. And because I knew them to be correct, there was no reason to change them.

I can't stress this enough: I was wrong. So very, very wrong.

Everything I'd thought was "natural instinct" was just projected, fearful bullshit doing nothing to bring me closer to my Authentic Self. Instead, it was locking me into an already-too-small world that didn't allow room for introspection, radical inquiry, or growth.

My world was unhappy. I was the sole creator of that unhappiness. But it wasn't until I started questioning my "rightness" that happiness was allowed to peek around the doorframe of my self-built house. As soon as I opened to the possibility of being wrong about *everything*, I was free to experience everything life had to offer.

What are you absolutely convinced you're right about?

Is it your religion? Are the books you read, the ideologies you subscribe to, and the phrases you repeat the *only* "right" ones? How can you be sure? Can you prove beyond a shadow of a doubt that your religion is "right" and everyone else's is wrong? (If you in all seriousness answered yes to those questions, please revisit Chapter 1 and remeet your Ego, because Authentic You can't honestly answer those questions with anything but an emphatic no. Of course, you can't prove your religion is "right." You can have unshakeable faith that it's right, but that's not the same thing.)

What about politics, beliefs about criminality and lawlessness, thoughts on gender and sexuality, parenting, marriage, social policies, and money? Does the belief in the rightness of these thoughts make us happy? Do we feel peaceful when we try to force those beliefs on others? Do we feel expansive when berating those who don't agree with us?

I don't expect you to agree with everything I say. I don't expect you to approve of everything I do. I do, however, hope you'll allow me the dignity and grace to experience my life on my terms, as I promise to extend to you the dignity and grace to do the same.

After all, I'd much rather be happy than be right.

The Ninth Practice: Question Everything

We've been practicing self-introspection throughout this book, so it should come as no surprise that the number one thing we can do on our journeys to becoming Good Humans is ceaselessly question our thoughts. It doesn't matter how normal we think the thought is. In fact, in the beginning, let's just assume none of our thoughts are Authentic, none of them are ours, and all of them need consideration.

Let's be ruthless in our self-introspection. Let's go a little crazy with it. Everything is fair game. *Ugh, I loathe [insert political commentator here]. Ew, broccoli is disgusting. I love being a parent. I can never quit my job.* Where did these thoughts come from? Who first taught us that we were supposed to loathe a certain person? When did we first decide to hate broccoli? Do we really love being a parent, all the time? Is it true we *can't* quit our job, or is it truer to say we're *afraid* to quit our job?

Once we're used to questioning every thought that comes through our head (and oh boy, do those thoughts love to come unbidden, all day long, 24/7, in a never-ending torrent), we can — and need to — move on to some of the harder stuff: The hard stuff is where real transformation begins.

- Why do I believe making it harder for some people to vote will make *me* safer?

- What am I resisting when I refuse to address the fears driving some people to question our election results?
- Why do I think wearing a mask in a global pandemic that's making hundreds of thousands of people sick is an affront to my individual freedom?
- What experiences has someone lived through who believes vaccinations are harmful?
- Why do I believe the color of someone's skin makes them inferior, or superior, in some way?
- What am I avoiding when I refuse to acknowledge racial divides?
- Why do I assume that police officers/pastors/my favorite politicians are always telling the truth?
- Why do I immediately discount the opinion of police officers/pastors/opposing politicians?
- Why do I get angry when someone disagrees with my viewpoint?
- Why am I uncomfortable at the idea of disagreeing with what others say is "common sense"?
- Where did I first learn the picture of what a "criminal" looks like?
- Why do I believe I'm only safe if all humans look, act, and think the same way I do?
- How do I feel about those who have money and wealth? Why?
- How do I feel about those who *don't* have money and wealth? Why?

There are myriad questions we can ask ourselves. And we need to be asking. Because right now, we — the collective, human we — are on the precipice of a terrible divide that's growing exponentially wider, deeper, and more treacherous every day we don't bother to ask these questions of ourselves and others.

Ruthlessly question yourself. Be brave enough to mine that ore. I promise, it's worth it, in a way that's immediately gratifying and beneficial. As soon as you're willing to ask the questions, amazing things happen: Growth. Space. Light. Connection. Everything you're craving but holding from yourself with your choice to remain divided into a camp of "us" or "them."

Remember your global family. Ask the hard questions. Return to wholeness.

We know now how to change our minds, and understand the importance of doing so. We realize genuine human connection can't occur without first investigating the shadiest parts of ourselves, acknowledge the world can't be changed without forging those connections, and recognize the direness of our situation if we don't start doing so immediately.

In the next chapter, we'll learn how it feels to move through the world Authentically, bravely, and in genuine curiosity. We'll put into motion all we've mastered about becoming a Good Human, and graciously invite our fellow human beings along for the ride.

11
The Arrival
Radicalize Your Authentic Self

I love that word. Radical. It's often misunderstood to mean something negative: The "radical" left or right in politics, or a so-called "radical" social movement, such as the democratic socialist leanings of the Black Panther Party or Movement for Black Lives.

To be *radical* is simply to be an advocate for change; to wish to leave behind what's historically been viewed as fundamental, but which is often nothing more than oppressive; and to deny the conservation of beliefs and policies that hinder rather than help forward progression.

My favorite definition of the word radical comes from Merriam Webster: "growing from the root of a plant, or from a stem that does not rise above the ground."

How beautifully symbolic is that? To be *radical* is to literally rise above the dirt that keeps us concealed: We don't detach ourselves completely from the root we sprouted from, but we do grow away from it to reach for light, water, and nutrients kept from us when buried.

Consider those layers of earth and dirt to be the thoughts, beliefs, and ideologies keeping us submerged. Yes, they've kept us rooted, perhaps even given us support when we thought we needed it, but now they're stifling our growth and denying our breath. So, we sprout off, forcing our way through the muck and mud, pushing aside soil until we break ground, creating our own radical branch of freedom.

Here, we recognize our thoughts are not us, and we are not our thoughts. They're still there, lurking underground, but we're no longer tethered to them. They gave us our first sustenance, but now we know: We can feed ourselves.

Breath and Body Break Free

Once, when strolling alongside my Padre, he observed me for a time and then said: "You hold your body so rigidly, like you're ready for battle. Do your neck and back hurt?" They did. And like everything else that becomes normalized, I thought it was just how bodies moved and felt. I didn't know to question my body's pain until it was pointed out to me as abnormal.

When we radicalize ourselves, we notice one thing first: We're no longer on guard. Our bellies have more room to take in and expel breath. Our shoulders relax. When we walk, we sway.

After many years of breathwork, yoga, hiking, and strength training, I know now that our bodies aren't meant to move through the world so stiffly. We're meant for running, jumping, rolling down hills, climbing up trees, cycling along country roads or commuter bike lanes, anything but the stiff-necked, low-back-cramped, hunched-over positions we find ourselves in modern working society. We're not meant to be standing for hours on an assembly line or sunk into a couch watching endless hours of Netflix. We're not meant to be lying on our backs squinting at tiny phone screens.

But the way we physically live our lives is only one part of our collective problem. We *are* ready for battle. We're ready with arguments, defenses, and critiques of all thoughts and beliefs different from our own. Our armor is constantly on, and it's heavy. It constricts our chests and throats, making it impossible to take a deep breath. And as we now know, breath must come first before freedom of any kind can be found.

Lay down your armor. It starts with your thoughts, but it ends in physical freedom. Be delighted by how freely your body moves when your mind is freely moving, too. You'll be amazed how few headaches, stiff necks, sore backs, and upset stomachs you experience once you've freed your mind.

Radicalize your mind. Your body will follow.

Energy Abounds

With this newfound mental and physical freedom comes something we possibly didn't realize we were missing. Energy. Like, jump-out-of-bed-at-6am-just-because-we-can kind of energy.

I used to hate mornings. It was only recently on my journey to becoming a Good Human that I realized it was because I didn't want to face what was waiting for me on the other side of sleep: monotony, anger, sadness, and joylessness. Why would I want to wake up and enter that world?

How do you wake up in the morning? Are you slow to get out of bed? Groggy? Grumpy? Stiff? Exhausted? These might be signs your Authentic Self isn't in charge of your autonomy — something or someone else is, and it's depleting your energy.

Can you honestly say you're *awake* after getting out of bed? There's a difference between moving zombie-style through life and being actively engaged with it. If it isn't a life you want to engage with — like mine before I removed my palm from in front of my face and exited my cave — then, my friend, you need to change it. This isn't about toxic positivity (the idea we can just ignore difficult or dangerous circumstances, think positively, and all will magically be well). Nor am I saying you need to start waking up at 5am to have a miracle morning. All I want you to do here is take a breath and ask yourself what needs to change for you to allow your lifeforce in.

Change one thing. Just one. Instead of getting out of bed and moving straight to the shower, pause. Stretch. Or recall one thing you're grateful for. Once that one change becomes the new habit, add another: Add a set of ten jumping jacks, or sit down to journal for 10 minutes. Once that habit is in rotation, add another. And another. Soon, without having to expend too much effort, your morning routine is something radically new, and once that radicalness has entered your world, I promise you're not going to want to live without it.

Where else can you drop in one new habit or change that will radicalize your routine? What about bedtime? How about your job? Your parenting? Your relationship? Your ministry?

See how it works? We push up through that grit and grime, sprout ourselves into a new form, and soon we're an altogether radical new entity.

Friendships Deepen

Have you ever watched a bucket of crabs? If not, Google it. It's amazing: A little crab will start to crawl toward the top of his writhing masses of brethren, clawing his way up and over each individual body to try to escape the bucket. Every excruciating step of the way his brother and sister crabs are desperately trying to yank him back down into the bucket, grabbing his legs, claws, and face to force him ever further downward. They don't want him to leave. They can't make it to the top and they don't want him to, either.

Maybe they're terrified of losing him because they count on him to bring home the bacon, er, algae, and don't want to be forced to rely on themselves for it. Perhaps they're afraid of what's outside the bucket and want to save him from whatever big, scary things he might find along his journey.

In our own lives, we're constantly being dragged back down into the bucket by our fellow humans. They don't want us to leave because they don't think *they* can leave, and that's unfair. They don't want us to leave because they're afraid they can't live without us. They don't want us to leave because they think the world is a scary place, so *we* should think it is, too.

121

None of these reasons is valid. All these reasons point to control — nothing more. If someone is pulling us down into the bucket, we must understand they're not helping us grow; they're holding back our growth. And if we hold someone back, can we honestly say we love and support them?

If someone is seeking to control us with guilt, shame, or commands, no matter how logically sounding the reason they give us might be ("I'm trying to protect you!"), we'll have to face the truth: This isn't a person looking out for our Authentic Self's best interest. And if we're seeking to control someone else, we'll have to face *this* ugly truth: We're *not* being a Good Human.

It feels scary at first, but every time we crawl up and over the rim of that bucket (or allow someone else to do so), we're opening the door for an even more amazing group of people to show up in our lives. We don't know them yet, and they don't know we're seeking them, but they'll find us. When they do, our world will blossom and change into something we couldn't have recognized before.

When I took my now-seemingly-requisite trip to Bali during my separation and eventual divorce from my ex-husband, I awoke one night in a sweat-soaked panic. My Ego thoughts were on overdrive: I can't survive without him! I don't make enough money! I won't be able to buy my kids clothes or food! Where are we going to live? What if he gets full custody? What if I get thrown in jail because some idiot judge believes all the nasty lies he's saying about me? What if they consider this month-long trip child abandonment? And on and on they spun.

I'm exhausted just rereading this. Because I was surrounded by people who'd been walking their Authentic paths for much longer than I had, I was encouraged to continue climbing out of my bucket rather than allowing myself to get pulled back in. I was reminded to practice using the tools I'd learned: Breath, first. Let the thoughts pass instead of settle. Question the statements.

I had to clear a path for new humans to show up for me. They couldn't arrive when my space was cluttered with bodies housing souls who didn't genuinely love, support, or see me. I had to leave them behind in their bucket and be willing to be on my own for a while before the universe was able to find me and send new, higher-consciousness companions.

Climb out of the bucket. Shake off the clingers. It's a radical act, yes. And it will literally change your world.

Fear of the Other Subsides

After we do this work for even a short time, something miraculous occurs: We realize we're no longer seeking to find the bad in others. We no longer fear their words or actions. We no longer consider them to be "other": They're an extension of us, so we treat them the way we treat ourselves.

Now, this prospect can be tricky if we're still stuck in egoic thought patterns, believing ourselves unworthy of respect, dignity, and love (if *we* don't deserve those things, we're not going to treat others as if *they're* deserving of them, either) or if we've not yet fully dissolved our egoic attachments to divisive belief systems.

But once we've brushed aside the Ego mind, patted it on its head like a well-behaved pet, and moved on to tend to our Authentic Selves, we remember with a rush of joy that we *are* worthy of receiving the bounty of the universe; therefore, we want everyone else to feel worthy and share in the abundance, too! Everyone includes those we previously thought undeserving; those we shunned, rejected, or ignored; and even our perceived enemies.

I struggled for the longest time with this. My ex-husband and his new wife were difficult people for me to forgive. I spent a very long time on my path to becoming a Good Human before I could genuinely say I wished them well. Too much hurt, too many lies and manipulations had flowed from them to me and my children, and forgiveness seemed a laughable goal.

When I got clear from my Ego mind surrounding these two humans, I was able to see I didn't *want* to forgive them: I was more committed to my self-righteous indignation than I was to being free and happy. I preferred to stay angry, which made me mean, less likeable and fun to be around, and depressed, which made me loathe them even more. What a horrible circle to be caught in!

My freedom from those chains didn't happen overnight. I did the hard, Ego-shattering work of getting very clear on how I'd attracted these two people into my life in the first place and what I'd done to court their criticisms. I looked good and hard at why I thought they needed to treat me a certain way and finally released myself from the bondage of their projections and my own expectations.

They are their business. I'm mine. As soon as I let that truth land, I was able to say, in all honesty and with love, "I wish these two people nothing but wellness and wholeness on their journey." They don't need to change. I do. They don't need to earn my respect. I do. They don't need to care. I do.

Who and what do we fear? Is it someone outside our faith who lives a lifestyle we've been trained to hate? Is it someone who sits on the corner near our office annoying us with their begging? Is it someone with a different skin color than ours, who dresses differently than we do, who speaks a language we don't understand? Is it someone who votes "the other way," who holds values we don't agree with and stands up for things we don't believe in?

Remember, there are two fields of energy we can choose to live in: Fear or Love. That's it. Fear will have us roaring in outrage or cowering in a corner, stuck in our muck, and rigidly clinging to invented lifelines. Love, however, will have us laughing in delight, creatively pondering the world around us, curiously questioning our thoughts and beliefs, and joyously inviting others in.

Love will shift our paradigm. Radically.

The Universe Provides

We're attuned to lack. None of us feels like we have enough. We need more money, always. We're convinced more money means a better life. For some, this is indisputably true. More money would mean stable, safe housing. It would mean nourishing food on the table. It would mean school supplies, warm coats in winter, and adequate healthcare.

For many of us, though, we already have more than enough. We own our homes or can comfortably pay our monthly rent. We get to choose between several grocery stores within a few miles of where we live and can afford the organic produce if we want it. We can dine out with friends, take vacations with our kids, and buy new clothes every season.

Yet we're convinced we don't have enough. We don't have what our neighbors have — a pool, a second car, a vacation home — and we certainly don't have what the really wealthy people in the lofty homes on the water have. So, we're always striving, working, grinding, and believing if we don't hustle to keep what's ours and get more of it, someone else will. They'll take what we've earned and keep us from getting a bigger piece of the pie.

I'm here to tell you this is nothing but a big stinking pile of bullshit.

The universe is abundant. It's wealthy beyond all measure. It has more to offer than most of us have yet realized. We don't have to worry about having enough, because we have all we need housed within us. We are enough. We always have been, and we always will be.

I'm talking about the power of an abundance mindset. I'm talking about manifesting that which we crave. And yes, I acknowledge how woo-woo that sounds, and how freakin' privileged it actually *is*.

When I was a single mom struggling to support two growing children with no child support in a teeny-tiny apartment and a low-paying job that didn't allow me to afford childcare, I wasn't thinking about how abundant and rich my life was and affirmation-ing myself into a better one. I was crying myself to sleep over the fact my teenage daughter had to share a room with her 5-year-old brother, that I couldn't afford to buy us a Christmas tree, and that I couldn't take my kids to their favorite restaurants for their birthday.

But I'm also here today as living proof that changing your mindset to one of abundance rather than lack does, in fact, work. It changes something on a molecular level: All your energy gets fired up to be shot out at something other than what you *don't* have. You start to see all you already *do* have, and even begin to catch glimpses of what's yet to come.

My shift to an abundance mindset came on a day where I'd just had enough: I was considering applying for welfare for the second time in my life to supplement a job that was barely paying enough for rent and gas money. I was exhausted from being wealth-less. I wanted an easier existence, for myself and my kiddos. I wanted to not worry so much.

I'd always desired a college degree but spent too much time telling myself the lies everyone tells themselves to avoid going for something big: I was too old to start, I couldn't afford it, I didn't have the time, I wasn't smart enough.

With these Ego beliefs screaming at me in a shrilling, panicked pitch, I walked through the doors of my local community college, gave the $25 I'd been planning on using for gas money to the registrar, and signed up to take a placement exam the very next day. I called my mom and asked her to pick up the kids from school. I didn't tell her why. I didn't tell anyone what I was doing, not until after I'd passed my exam and been placed in English 101 and remedial math, not until I'd pored painstakingly over the class selection list and nervously filled out my FAFSA, not until after I'd won several scholarships for single mothers over the age of 35 that paid fully for my school. Then, I let everyone in.

My universal support has never abated, not once since I took that one quiet, giant step toward my dream.

The universe provides. It provides for everyone. It provides more than we could ever need. We do, however, have to be available to receive it. We need to be willing to walk away from fear and into courage to accept it. We must be willing to do whatever it takes, all the Ego-shattering work, to tap into it. We must be willing to leave behind our old beliefs, idols, and ideologies. We must be willing to walk away from the ones we thought we loved, and who we thought loved us, to journey along the only path that can truly be ours. We must be willing to be called names, shunned, misunderstood, divorced, and disowned. We must be willing to die, to let our Ego drown, to give up who we thought we knew ourselves to be to become the Authentic person we're meant to be. We must be prepared to get a little radical.

We must do these things to truly call ourselves Good Humans.

Are you ready?

Epilogue
The Final Practice

One of the first pieces of advice I received when I began my Good Human journey was this: "Whatever you would normally do, do the opposite."

This is pretty sage wisdom. After all, if we've been operating entirely from Ego, it stands to reason that our actions (which stem from our thoughts) have been, at the very least, incorrect, and at their worst very damaging, not only to ourselves but to all those around us as well.

So, once we wake up to the fact this voice in our head, which we thought was our best friend, has been running our mindless show, doesn't it make sense we won't want to take the same actions/think the same thoughts/engage in the same behaviors we did before we knew we'd been bamboozled? Of course it does!

Our Ego mind exists separately from our Authentic Self. Once we allow this truth to land, to know it in our bones and live from it exclusively, we have a seemingly gargantuan task ahead of us: to be ever on the lookout for our triggers and begin to piece together for ourselves what our habitual responses are so that, in each moment, we can instead choose anew.

Ego wants us to stay in the dark. It wants us to stay "safe," which, in this case, is code for "Don't change. Don't rock the boat. Don't stand out. Don't be different. Don't want more. Don't think you deserve more. Don't go after more. Don't be more." If this is what Ego wants, and we know now that we don't want to feed our Ego, what does it mean to do the opposite?

Basically, anything you're used to doing, stop doing. Immediately.

Are you a late riser? Get up an hour earlier. Do you usually turn on the TV after dinner? Take a walk instead. Do you only engage with certain groups on social media? Find new ones. (Better yet, don't turn on social media at all!) Have you gotten up religiously every Sunday to be at church by 9am? Don't go this weekend.

Did any of those challenges bring up emotion for you? Awesome! You're on the right track! You know what to do: Breathe. Ask yourself a genuinely curious question. Let it drop into your consciousness and take note of what arises.

Huh. Why did my chest and throat tighten, and my spine stiffen, when I thought about not going to church this weekend? or *What do I think is going to happen if I don't go to church this weekend?* or *Who do I think is going to be upset with me if I don't go to church this weekend?* Now, maybe for you, it's the exact opposite. Maybe going to church is the very thing you should do because a genuinely inclusive support system is there that can help you excavate your attachments and get you unstuck from your ideologies. Maybe there are people there who love you enough to challenge your thinking, and it's that very challenge that's kept you from attending the last several weeks.

If you're someone who tends to react with anger when someone disagrees with you, next time try staying quiet and listen actively to the person speaking. If you traditionally shy away from confrontation, challenge yourself to speak up when you see or hear something said or done that's harmful or false. If you're used to only watching one news station, change the channel and see what's being discussed elsewhere.

Walk your radical new path, bravely and with curiosity. You, showing up Authentically, will give permission for others to do the same. In this way, we facilitate change to what lies outside of us: the world we must live in and the humans we get to live alongside.

❀

What does it mean to be attached? It means being tethered, anchored to something. It's a weight that holds us down, holds us back, keeps us from moving freely.

I want you untethered. That's the only way to be truly free. The cool thing is when we free ourselves, we automatically set others free, as well. And that's the greatest gift we could ever give another human being.

What are you attached to? And how can you tell?

Well, what are some of your long-held beliefs? We become very comfortable in our beliefs; they feel like home. They're what we "know" to be true, and we can't imagine budging one inch from them. That refusal to budge is attachment. That stubborn, inflexible, rigid, stiff-jawed, tensed-up bracing of our body that means we're ready to throw down and defend what we "know" is "right," come hell or high water.

But beliefs are nothing more than ideas we individually generated (along with the help of societal norms and expectations), then decided to embrace and believe in wholeheartedly. They've become part of what we term our "personalities" — which, we now know, is really just our Egos — and so it feels uncomfortable to question them, let alone take a breath and say out loud, "You know, maybe this simply isn't true."

We don't have to change what we choose to believe in. We just need to be open to the idea our beliefs may not, in the end, be correct. This is a fundamental truth that's true for all of us, regardless of what we believe.

❦

There are only two states of being we humans can choose to operate from: Fear, and Love. Love is the place we wish we were living in and acting from, all the time. But Fear is the place we most often reside. Think of what typically motivates us to action: How do government officials inspire us to vote? How do religious leaders convince us of our righteousness? How do journalists get us to click on their headlines? By instilling in us a fear of the "other."

We instinctively fear what we don't know. And that fear, when left unexamined, solidifies into judgment, attack, projection, tribalism, and nativism. These, in turn, are what give rise to genocide, holocausts, ethnic cleansings, and the caging of human bodies. This isn't hyperbolic. After all, could

Love conceive of things like jail, war, slavery, or laws that strip human beings of autonomy?

Ego operates from Fear. Authenticity springs forth from Love. These are the only choices, but they *are* choices. How will you choose to exist in the world?

❀

Life isn't all or nothing. We like to pretend our experiences in the world are linear and binary, but they're not. Individuals and groups of human beings can't *always* or *never* be anything. All we can be is human, which means we're sometimes magnificent, oftentimes ordinary, and every so often total shits. But always we're doing the best we can with the tools we were given and beliefs we picked up along the way.

❀

When you're truly free from Ego, you can admit cheerfully you know *nothing.* You know *no one.* You really don't even know your Authentic Self — *yet.* And rather than feeling terrified or burdened by this, you feel delighted, giddy even, at all that's yet to be discovered in you, your new world, and the human beings surrounding you.

Freedom for all from idols and ideologies. Now *that* is a radical way to exist in the world.

Thank You for Reading *The Good Human*!

If you enjoyed the practices introduced in this book and believe they will benefit others, please take a moment to **write an honest review** on Amazon.

Your input is valuable and genuinely appreciated.

Let's connect!

www.dawnkhammer.com

 @WriterDawnH

 @writer.dawn.h

 @ writerdawnh

Acknowledgments

I'd like to thank the team at Self-Publishing School, who work tirelessly and with great faith to help first-time authors such as myself bring our dreams to life. Thank you especially to Chandler Bolt, Jordyn Moore, Kerk Murray, Sean Sumner, Ellaine Ursuy, and Rachael Williams, who each helped prod me along this long and winding path with words of encouragement and examples of jobs well done.

To my editor, Wayne Purdin, I am forever indebted. Your on-point critiques and sometimes not-so-gentle nudging helped make this book the best version it could be, and they challenged my own egoic ideologies. Jeannie Culbertson, your patient answers to my endless questions about formatting and willingness to sprinkle those extras into my pages made this book something beautiful to behold. Thank you both.

To the army of friends and family who read the early versions of my chapters, donated funds to get me started, and believed in my message even when I didn't — thank you doesn't feel adequate. This offering wouldn't exist without you. I'm blessed.

Finally, to my long-suffering husband; our beautiful, inquisitive children; my anxiety-fueled pup Berkeley; and my parents, thank you for your unwavering faith and steadfast love. You're the ones inspiring me to become the very best Good Human I can be.

Xoxo,
DK

About the Author

Dawn K. Hammer is a writer currently cohabiting with her husband, teenage son, and sweetly neurotic rescue pup along the shores of Puget Sound in the Pacific Northwest. Recently graduated from the University of Washington with dual degrees in Law and Policy and Communication at the tender young age of 43, she's finally pursuing her lifelong dream of getting paid to write for a living. *The Good Human* is her first published book.

Want more from the practices offered in *The Good Human*? Visit

https://www.subscribepage.com/the-good-human

to access your free printable action guide and journal.